THE

I CANT HEAR

HARDEST

I CANT SEE

LANGUAGE

I CANT SPEAK

Carmelo Rodriguez

The Hardest Language
Copyright © 2020 by Carmelo Rodriguez
All Rights Reserved

All rights reserved. No part of this publication may be reproduced, distributed, or transmitted in any form or by any means, including photocopying, recording, or other electronic or mechanical methods, without the prior written permission of the AUTHOR, except in the case of brief quotations embodied in critical reviews and certain other noncommercial uses permitted by copyright law. This book is intended for educational purposes only.

Publisher: Absolute Author Publishing House
Editor: Dr. Melissa Caudle
Junior Editor: Paul L. Dupre
Cover Designer: Rebecca @Rebeccacovers

LIBRARY OF CONGRESS CATALOGUE IN-PUBLICATION-DATA

The Hardest Language/Rodriquez, Carmelo

p. cm.

Paperback ISBN: 978-1-64953-113-1
eBook ISBN: 978-1-64953-114-8

1. Policing 2. Communication 3. Educational

TO ALL THE MEN AND WOMEN IN BLUE!

TABLE OF CONTENTS

Introduction i

Chapter 1 1

THE MOST POWERFUL WEAPON 1

Chapter 2. 15

The Path to Peace 15

Chapter 3. 30

Processing the Information 30

Chapter 4. 43

Police Force and Police Shootings 43

Chapter 5 57

Talk to Me 57

Chapter 6. 67

Understanding and Practicing Non-Verbal Cues 67

Chapter 7 85

Understand and Respond 85

Chapter 8 97

What would you do? 97

Chapter 9 108

Where your power lies 108

Chapter 10 117

The Last Resort 117

Chapter 11 130
Community Policing 130
Chapter 12 144
Emotional Intelligence 144

Introduction

A common phenomenon that almost anyone will agree with is the sense of apprehension between the city, law enforcement officers, and our citizens. This apprehension dates back to time immemorial. I don't have the data, but I am sure it's been like that ever since the beginning of the concept of maintaining peace and law and order in any society. This conception is held throughout all civilization as long as man and his peers are involved.

Now, what the root cause of the apprehension is, no one may know. However, it often reflects in our culture, race, the idea of the privileged and the oppressed. Then again, I believe and challenge that these things may not be the root cause.

Now, I am not seeking to make light of these significant problems as they do not exist; however, what I am saying, in essence, is that no one knows why it exists; thus, it makes things signification more complicated. It's almost as though when you turn on the news, there are scores of law enforcement versus civilian cases that may escalate into terrible episodes of different violent acts. These acts often lead to loss of life, properties, and vandalism to state- and privately-owned properties. When considered, one begins to question what the real problem is and how to solve it.

I think it would be myopic to consider these problems in the light of gender, race, sociocultural values, and politically engineered biases alone. Why? It will not be fair to look at it as a problem that occurs only in the United States because it's a big issue that cuts across nationalities and creed. I like to think of it more as a human-centric problem. As such, I believe it can only be solved when everyone, law enforcement, and citizens alike take the initiative to create a better environment that fosters safety and supports everyone's peaceful growth in the community.

In trying to think through the problem, I concluded that perhaps the challenge could be in the genetic makeup and design in man himself because no one created likes to be boxed by a set of rules and regulations. We all love to be free and exercise our rights to freedom and do anything we like. However, we want to do things without restrictions so much that once a regulation is introduced, our default setting kicks in to test the limit of the restriction and see what happens if we ever exceed it.

The truth is this trait can be detected as early as the childhood experiences, where you tell a child not to do something, and then you discover that what you instructed shouldn't be done is what the child wants to do; the Christian Bible puts it this way:

> "...Nevertheless, I would not have known what sin is had it not been for the law. For I would not have known what coveting really was if the law had not said, 'You shall not covet'" *(Romans 7:7).*

This resonates, right? Haven't you ever wondered that inscriptions such as "Do Not Touch" actually stir up a curiosity in you that makes you want to touch whatever it is? Here is why. The real sense of it, as humans, we will always allow our curiosity to get the best of us; if not, there won't be scientific breakthroughs and other significant advancements and achievements that humanity has been able to attain.

Are we then going to say that having human curiosity is bad? No! I believe that curiosity is a type of measurement, which means that we have massive and limitless potential to unlock great things. Still, its effectiveness is dependent on the host; that is, the person who harbors the emotion and curiosity as it were.

In my book, *Race Against Your Alarm Clock,* I mentioned that the idea of a box was put in place to create a balanced environment for everyone to operate with a standard regulation that promotes fairness and growth as defined and agreed upon by a community. In this book's context, the box can be the law, and the community can be a country, state, or international bodies depending on the breadth of the scope. The community decides to empower a few people within it to serve as those who will help uphold and enforce the fair agreed-upon guidelines, and herein lies the beginning of the challenge.

The people empowered to ensure compliance with the statutory law are a human representation of the agreed-upon law and precepts. They are empowered to act in the community's capacity *for the community*, which is the people in the first place. The empowered people may sometimes not see each other in the light of what they represent; that is the law and the one that needs protecting.

Instead, we see ourselves as individuals and the statutes created as an abstract that limits us from freedom of expression; and this causes a huge divide and births the violence that we experience between the law enforcement and the community, such that when someone errs, and law enforcement comes at them. They don't see it for what it is; the law has been flaunted, thereby causing unfairness to someone, and damaging the balance of peace for others in the community. Instead, they see the individual behind the uniform and pour the aggression they nurture that stems from the disdain of the limits placed on them by the [limits set by the] law on him.

In the same vein, the one meant to uphold the law sees the person who flaunts the law as the disturber of the peace and a disruptor. Still, the challenge is that rather than seeing the situation for what it is, which is don't box in people, he completely forgets about human behavior and responds [most times] not as the law, but as a pissed individual because someone has a disregard for the law.

However, this is where the complication starts: because rather than allowing the law to take its course, he [the law enforcer] begins to react based on human emotions and antecedents based on his encounters, misguided beliefs, and interactions with the people in the community. For example, a history of crime rates and the volatility of an area to violent cases may inform an officer's response to criminal cases in a community, such that areas with lesser crime rates may see their law enforcers respond in a milder way to violators while those in areas with a high crime rate respond with a more brutal force.

Again, I will say that this is not a function of race, religion, or gender, as that will be equivalent to nipping a bud while not being mindful of the root as it were. Instead, it is a function of having a crucial understanding of who we are and where we fit in the scheme of things -- both as law enforcement and citizens—then having the boldness to hold essential conversations between both parties that will eventually lead to us joining our collective forces to build a peaceful society that won't just be habitable to us but will also be a haven for generations.

I believe so strongly that to attain this peace and unity we need in our society (or any society or community around the world), willing to indulge in some crucial conversations that will help take the bull by the horn to become harmonious living between the law and the people it seeks to protect. Yes, that also includes law enforcement officers.

I will be directing the conversation toward the men in uniform, especially as touching how to communicate effectively and have critical conversations, first with themselves as individuals and then with the community they serve. I will seek to amplify the necessities for a healthy conversational style, especially concerning de-escalating a volatile situation and people hoping for a greater level of peace attained in our communities.

The truth is, being a Latino, I know what it feels like to have a terrible background and to be in the midst of those who take pleasure in pushing boundaries in the name of doing what is right by them. This behavior is usually at the expense of the community. I know how this reality has shaped their mentality about law enforcement, especially the *Men in Blue,* thereby leading to a heightened apprehension level.

I am currently serving in a police department, having been a soldier deployed to the middle east, and then came back to service in this capacity (first coming from a correctional then into the policing background). I can tell you that I know the fears and struggles officers go through, especially in communities with high crime rates.

I hope to bridge the divide by helping officers of the law to communicate what may look like the most challenging conversations to have in the line of duty in the easiest possible way.

The big idea this book represents is basically about sharing effective communications principles in a way that transcends the social divide and seeks to amplify understanding amongst parties involved in conversations. I will be drawing inference from the law enforcement perspective by helping them understand all forms of communication, both verbal and non-verbal cues, and identify the various threat levels of conversations from the citizens' viewpoint.

The Mistake People Make in Communicating

Often, the mistake we make when trying to have conversations is, we take a one-cap-fits-all approach. The outcome often escalates situations where they become uncontrollable to the point that it disturbs the very peace of the community we are trying to protect.

I must give credit to the government and law enforcement agencies here in the United States who have invested so much in teaching officers of the law on different emotional intelligence courses and addressed practical communication issues based on the diverse demography and human realities. I believe strongly that the law officers have more part to play running with the ideologies taught, as most people get to see that there's a whole world of difference between theories and practices.

One of the things that I know is needed is the fundamental skill of communicating effectively, which I believe is a phenomenon that we, as individuals, have lost, and it has escalated into our communities. People lack the discernment required to pass messages across as we have become somewhat self-absorbed in our realities that we neglect others' needs and those trying to reach out to us.

For example, have you ever thought that the same way you are thinking about what to say to your partner or neighbor is also the same way they think about what to say to you? Funny, right? But really, it is the truth.

Some time ago, I listened to a *Ted Talk* by Celeste Headlee on having a good conversation. She listed ten things one shouldn't do when having conversations, and I will share them here, but in addition to the points she gave, I will seek to elaborate it a little bit.

1. **Don't Multi-task** - You know how you are having a conversation with someone, and you are not present because you are probably thinking about something else, or you're on your phone while the other party is talking, and he's trying to get your attention? That hurts and communicates to the other person that you'd rather they don't speak! As she advised, it's better to end a conversation if you won't be all into the conversation.

2. **Don't Pontificate** - True listening is all about setting your opinion aside to hear the other party and understand their intentions. You shouldn't approach any conversation on a high horse. Instead, be open-minded, knowing that there's always something to learn.

3. **If You Need to Ask Questions, Use Open-Ended Questions** - I'm sure you've heard the phrase, "Every question always has an answer." While that may be true in life, I believe it doesn't represent the whole truth in conversations; instead, it should read, "Every question asked rightly always has an answer."

4. **Go with The Flow** - You know how people can break the flow of conversations because they aren't listening to you? The person you're speaking to is probably talking about pizza, and then while in the middle of the conversation, you thought about something amazing. I won't deny that, and then you just cut in abruptly, or you take the conversation in a whole different tangent. That's not fair, and it communicates absent-mindedness and doesn't make the other person feel valued.

5. **If You Don't Know, Say That You Don't Know; Err on The Side of Caution -** You don't have to be under any form of pressure to please anyone about the wealth of knowledge you have on any subject matter. Sometimes it's noble not to have all the answers and then own up to the fact that you don't. I can bet it with you that you will be more respected for it.

6. **Don't Equate Your Experience with Theirs; It Is Never the Same** - You need to understand that all experiences are unique for different individuals even if the situations are similar; therefore, it is not about you. Once you tow the path of equating your experience with that of a grieving person or the person talking to you, you might unknowingly sound condescending and make it look as though you've hijacked the conversation. You need to bear in mind that conversations are not a promotional activity.

7. Try Not to Repeat Yourself - A whole lot of people do this! I believe that one of the most effective ways to have conversations is always to keep it simple; there's no point over stressing a point when it could've been said just once, and then you move on! Stop rephrasing it!

8. Stay Out of The Wins - Let people enjoy themselves in the spotlight, too. You don't always have to hijack the conversation and make it all about yourself. Yes, you're vital, but let people get the shine too.

9. Listen - No man has ever listened his way out of a job. It probably takes more effort to listen and be present than it does to talk, but you must listen well to have effective conversations. (I will talk more on the subject of listening in upcoming chapters).

10. Be Brief - Never attempt to over-flog a point you are trying to make because it sounds so cool to your hearing!

Chapter 1

THE MOST POWERFUL WEAPON

Suppose there's anything I really and truly love about the times we live in right now. In that case, it is the fact that unlike any other era humanity has ever known, we are now more connected and more intertwined than before, especially when we consider life in the light and beauty of cross-culture and dynamism.

It's no news that people and systems now merge seamlessly with statistics showing that over a hundred million messages are sent via instant messaging apps and social media platforms. As a matter-of-fact economist now refers to the world as a global village, a term that underscores the level of connectivity that we humans share amongst each other.

For example, just a little over a century ago, technology's advent wasn't as advanced as we have it now. One may argue that more had to be said to pass across a piece of information in terms of communication. People had time on their hands, even though I believe that every generation always had the same idea about time. In retrospect, the generation coming after will always view the preceding generation in the light of people having more quality time to spend with each other and time to live life more simply.

It was easier to enjoy life together as a family and truly connect soul-to-soul and go on dates without worrying about things going wrong; they generally had time to connect and bond well. Take, for example, messaging. Suppose I were to send mail to someone who was miles away from me. I'd probably take my time to send a detailed message because I know I may not have the luxury to send snail mail frequently (still talking about fifty to a hundred years ago. I don't even want to bother what a thousand years ago looked like), so I will have to detail my message in such a way that the receiver could understand my intentions and message clearly. Oh, and when we get to see, I will make sure that I try as much as possible to say a whole lot clearer and answer any question the person might have because I need to take advantage of the little time connection can give me.

Not that I was around then. Well, none of us were but studying the communication pattern in those times. We will see these traits in their messaging and message quality.

However, with the advent of a borderless world through technological advancements, messaging has become very easy, as humans have discovered a way to say more with less time with the advent of mobile phones and other communication devices. Herein lies the problem -- the fact that more is said does not mean that more is communicated. Communication isn't complete if there isn't an understanding of the information passed.

One of the most cherished and most crucial essences of human existence is the need for connection and interaction. Humans were not created to live in isolation. I dare say that we find the true essence of our existence and definition in our ability to connect with the people around us and impact [or be impacted by] the surrounding people. Communication plays a critical role in communicating values, ideologies, feelings, emotions, and intentions.

Human communication is imparting or exchanging Information from one person to another through the use of languages [and different media] in such a way that the true intent of the information [as conceived by the informant] is made known to the receiver [the party being communicated to]. However, communication isn't complete until the informee gives [satisfactory] feedback to the initiator, as this shows that the message was well received and understood.

Now, because human connection is a major driving force in the makeup and structure of life, communication plays a central and integral role in connecting us and achieving that essence of existence. Think of life as a giant web made up of different dots and connecting strands. Then, picture it so that people worldwide, irrespective of their creed, race, ideologies, and belief systems, are the different dots and endpoints in the web structure; then picture the strands as the connection we all must form with each other.

If you picture it this way, you will discover that although one endpoint may be connected to either two or four other endpoints. What gives the web its shape is the connecting strands between the dots, lest there isn't a web anymore. It is the same with life. We all take our essence from our understanding of who we are and the strength of our connection to the surrounding people. Now, more critical than the connecting strands is a factor most people fail to consider is the strength of the web, which is dependent on the strength of the connecting strands. That strength of the connecting strand is what communication brings to the mix. It is safe to say that the quality of connection we share amongst each other depends on the strength of our ability to communicate and interact with each other.

When we choose to see and understand life in light of this reality, we will discover that a lot of work needs to be devoted to ensuring that we communicate better as humans. This understanding strengthens the bond we share so much that life's quality becomes better when the bond is strong, where I have a reservation with technology.

I, for one, don't think technology concerning creating human connectivity is at fault here. Instead, I believe that we are losing the very essence of the connection we share when we reduce social interaction to technological mediation alone, as seen by the degree of insensitivity to emotions portrayed by many people around us today.

Humanity interacts in such a way that we all, even though different as individuals, should only attain completion and fulfillment when we interact with one another by bringing our unique individuality into the mix to make a beautiful collage of personalities and ideas keeps the world going—as such, attaining this can only be achieved with the strength of our interactions.

The Weight of Words

One of the things that makes human interactions unique is our ability to give voice to our thoughts by shaping them into spoken words that often transcribes the energy and the feelings within us to an understandable format that the people around [and close to] us can understand and respond to something communications experts call verbal and non-verbal cues.

Spoken words are carriers of energy as they carry the weight of our most authentic and most profound feelings and articulate it in such a way that people around us feel and understand the things that we want to say but aren't saying. A spoken word can reflect inner longings and deep desires to a receiver so that the purpose and intent are understood and given a proper response.

When it comes to human interaction, I believe effective communication clarifies the receiver more than text messaging. In the former, you can hear intentions and expressions, while the latter is purely subject to the receiver's prejudice based on many factors like the person's idea of you and his or her state of the heart.

For example, have you ever received a message from a friend and read it with a mental bias based on your knowledge of your friend's character, only for you to see him [or her] and you have the conversation again? This time you get more clarity on what the person was saying.

That's what I'm insinuating here. More effective than spoken words are physical interactions. It opens you up totally to the unchecked flood of emotions amplified by lots of verbal and non-verbal cues embedded in conversations.

However, the challenge is that somewhere along the line of human existence, we have lost the art of conversing and communicating our true intents effectively. It feels as though people are celebrated for masking their emotions and showing off a form of maturity by saying nice things at the detriment of the truth about their feelings. At the other end of the spectrum are those who don't have the finesse to articulate their words correctly and infuse every word with a flood of emotions. For example, anger and rage erupt, and people speak things that should never even be said at all.

Words are vital and powerful, as they are a flection of one's real intent. Most people know but don't understand that words cannot be unsaid. Even when you apologize for saying something wrong and out of turn, you will still have to bear the brunt, depending on its weight and to whom the words were spoken.

For example, it's common to see people being held accountable for comments they passed several years ago, mostly because the advent of technology has made data storage easy and accessible to everyone. One needs only to click the keypad or touch of a mobile device to find out loose comments made against creeds and races; even gender comes back to bite people in the face. Remember, words cannot be unsaid, neither recalled. I see it as an energy that stays on in life, waiting to be activated again.

We need to understand that words are powerful, so much so that no matter how long ago they were spoken, embedded in them is the same force of potency, and nothing will take it away. If anything, the longer words stay, the more apparent the potency and intent remain known. Let me make you see it this way; if you look at ancient texts and scrolls, especially across religious and philosophical texts, one can't help but wonder how millions of people decided to live their lives by the dictates of the words spoken by the gods, God, prophets, and philosophers thousands of years ago.

Don't get me wrong. I am not against religion or philosophy, as I believe in the concept of ideologies and know that these texts are insights for having a richly successful life and attaining peace and serenity.

Also, read biographies and study ancient civilizations. You will discover that words govern the world in itself – kingdoms have toppled, and dynasties have ended or begun on the strength of a collection of words. Wars have started or ended by the speaking loose or sweet words, and many people have been convicted or set free basically on the strength of words. Like I said earlier, embedded in every word are true intentions and energies (or vital forces) residents in the carrier, the person who spoke them.

If then words are this powerful and can change the course of history, then don't you think we need to learn to be conscious and master the art of saying the right words at the right time for the right situation? The force of words governs the world – some spoken by the right people; issues have been escalated out of control because someone said something out of turn, or sometimes because the person meant to say something chose to stay silent. Oh, let's not forget that families have also started on the strength of words, and people's trajectory altered at the power of the word spoken either in season or out of turn. For something, this important and significant, we must teach ourselves how to convey the right word – and this is where the art of communicating comes in.

I believe so strongly that when we all learn how to speak words that are well-seasoned with wisdom and understanding. Then, the conversations we will be having – healing conversations that will play a huge part in healing the hurting a d strengthening the divides in our communities – these conversations will become smoother and birth the changes we so much desire.

As an officer of the law, I passionately believe that mastering the art of speaking the right words to the people in the surrounding community is essential, especially seeing the recent volatility and negative bias the community may have toward us. I understand that sometimes we feel that the people we are called to serve can be insensitive to our emotions, too, as they tend to think we have all the answers and that we need to do more. It's the burden of expectation, as I always like to put it, especially when people are oblivious to the fact that we are humans and are only empowered by the law, even though that doesn't immune us from life's struggles.

I understand how it feels to be feared by those we are called to protect and love, which eventually leads to them not trusting us as they ought to; but then again, that's not where it stops as we also have those who look down on us with a condescending approach, almost as though they tag us as a bunch of "low-lives" that are fragile and require help because they feel we couldn't get something better out of life and policing is our escape route;

Trust me, I understand both of these views and differing opinions about our work. Still, these realities don't deter us from doing what is right irrespective of the situations and circumstances. We must learn how to insulate ourselves and up the ante on our communication ethics so much so that when we are in the line of duty, the responsibility that we have taken up to improve on ourselves will set us apart and will further help promote peace and tranquility in the communities that empowered us to serve and protect.

For example, I have some basic guiding principles that I live by when it comes to me saying anything to anyone in whatever capacity I find myself in, and I would like to share them with you here:

1. I seek to know and understand myself. Before I engage in any form of conversation, I try as much as possible to know and understand my frame of mind and the state which I am in so as not to bleed on someone who knew nothing about my cut or, better put, so as not to transfer aggressions unnecessarily.

I believe that every conversation has a required tone, and a persona required to communicate effectively. As such, a preset frame of mind is needed to intentionally stir the discussion for the greater good, as defined by the purpose and the intention of the conversation.

For example, to have a conversation that is meant to foster peace between two or more people, one cannot afford to be the hot-headed. As such, you may have to do more of a soul-search to know if you are in the best position to mediate because most times, we get to project our personalities and consciousness into the conversations we have.

2. I try as much as possible to know if I have enough information or mastery about the subject matter. One of the mistakes most people make when entering conversations is that they trivialize the importance of having the right information and understanding all the puzzle pieces that make the whole.

I have come to learn that before I speak, mediate or air my opinion about any conversation or matter, I need to have enough information about the subject. It may not be to the level of professorial mastery, but you need to have all your facts right, and when you don't, it is better to be upfront about it and let the people you are talking to know that you don't have the complete information.

3. I seek to know and understand where the people (or person) stand on the subject matter. I have seen several people make the mistake of not caring about what people they are in talks with think about a subject or an ideology, and that usually ends up in offense and strife, and in some cases may lead to community unrest that may escalate into something uncontrollable.

I find this to be a particularly important principle when dealing with anyone or a group of people who share a common belief system. For example, I think it will be chaotic to go to the LGBTQ community and denounce them right to their faces because you do not share their sexuality views. In the same vein, it will be wrong to incite a Muslim community and infer that they are a group of violent extremists.

I have discovered people want to be heard and believe that their opinion supersedes that of the other person or group. Because of this, they always seek to direct conversations to soothe their preconceived narrative. Most of them don't know that the general feeling might be that of strife and discontent at the end of the conversation. However, only a few people understand that when it comes to communication, the receiver's ability to understand and comprehend what is said is equally important as the message – if not more, as such as the carrier of the message, more emphasis needs to be placed on the heart and capacity of the receivers – of what use is trying to explain the concept to trigonometry to kindergarten?

These three basic guidelines are what I have been able to use as principles to communicating effectively and honestly; it has saved me a whole lot of stress, not only on the line of duty but also in my business relations and even families because I like to think of them as principles.

I firmly believe that principles are universal because they are not restricted to a particular line of expression, situation, or circumstances; that is what works in policing can also work for business development and client relations.

SUMMARY

1. Human communication is simply the imparting or exchange of information from one person to another through the use of languages [and

different media] in such a way that the true intent of the information [as conceived by the informant] is made known to the receiver [the party being communicated to].

2. Words are loaded with vital energy forces and will always stay in the atmosphere to either work for you or against you as you journey through life.

3. Before you communicate with anyone about a particular subject matter, you need to:
    a. Understand and know yourself well.
    b. Know if you have enough information on the subject matter.
    c. Know and understand where the person (or people) stand on the subject.

Chapter 2.

The Path to Peace

You can die if you use the wrong words. Yes, it is that serious! You can get sued and get your own life spiraling out of control from the use of inappropriate comments sputtering out of your mouth. At the same time, with the power embedded in your words, you can be the cream of the crop and shape your life in such a way that you perpetually progress in an upward tangent that guarantees you have a good and fruitful life. Whichever way you want it, the power of choice lies within you, as expressed by the words you say.

THE HARDEST LANGUAGE

When it comes to having conversations, especially in the line of duty, one of the truths that people often realize is that it's effortless for conversations to spiral out of control and degenerate to the point of civil unrest and loss of life. I am sure you might've heard or even witnessed or been in situations where what began as a simple conversation, or even an arrest, ended up in several violent acts, even shootings or gang wars.

When it comes to human relations, we need to understand that everyone looks out for themselves, which fuels their expectations. It doesn't just stop there. This predisposition almost always leads us to say things that we most likely may not correctly think through; after all, we live in a world filled with a larger percentage of people who are usually not in the habit of thinking things through before saying them.

I know that most people (if you can go through the stress of asking if they feel they know how to say the right words at the right time) will give you an answer in the affirmative, but the reality [as expressed by what we see around us] doesn't support this answer. It points out that most people, out of their need to be heard, believe they are always right. They know how to talk well, and hardly anyone will admit that they have a lot of work to do to improve how they communicate with [and to] the surrounding people.

To drive this point further home, I will be talking about this matter in the concept of the two kinds of languages that people use when communicating with others.

The first is the natural language, which is our default mode of speaking. At its peak, it is a simple way of talking, and I will say that it is characterized by being unpolished and all too expressive; you know that kind of language used that is uncensored when you tend to say things the way they are without holding back your feelings and emotions. The truth is that the natural language at its best can be disastrous and tends to incite hurt and pain. I may not be able to delve into the why in this book, but the truth is natural language isn't refined.

Then there's the tactical language, which is the refined way of talking characterized by the amount of thoughtfulness a speaker puts into constructing his sentences to pass his message across in the best possible way to elicit the kind of response(s) wanted from the receiver. The use of tactical language (as the name infers) requires an extraordinary level of intentionality. It is usually against the norm of the human response to thinking through words, mainly when emotions express heightened feelings. The idea of tactical language is about taking a step back from how you feel and considering matters from every possible angle. You dissect the situation, the variants of probable actions, and form your response based on what you want to see.

THE HARDEST LANGUAGE

According to Academic-turned-cop and bestselling author George Doc Thompson, he categorizes natural language as unprofessional, express personal feelings, uses self-referencing languages like "I" or "Me." In other words, a user that engages in allowing himself always to be guided by the dictates of the natural language has more propensity to finding himself in situations that he cannot always control. In contrast, tactical languages are professional, require intentional use of words to achieve its purpose, employ simple communication in target, and try as much as possible to contact its intended audience.

Natural languages are always disastrous, and you cannot bring it back. I once heard an African proverb from a friend that says, "Words are like eggs," more like the proverbial *Humpty Dumpty* such that once spoken, all the King's men will never be able to put it together again.

By nature, humans are creatures of energy, and what we call human interactions is a transference of energy from one person to the other. The thing about energy transference in humans (as with science) is that energy transfers from a high concentration region to a lower concentration, a phenomenon tagged as infection.

Have you ever contacted a friend, and then you discover that the whole mood around you changes? Have you ever ridden in a bus with someone or met another person at the pack and then find that there's a lot of energy [either toxic energy or excitement] that burst from them? Before you know it, you begin to imitate (or reflect) their energy? And sometimes, it could be the other way round, as you may be the one to give off the energy as it were.

What I am saying, in essence, is that every one of us has a unique energy signature that follows us around like a cologne infecting the surrounding people. The unique thing about this energy is that one of the primary vehicles it transmits is that the words we speak are reflected by the language we use, either natural or tactical.

As an officer of the law, you need to understand this reality and know that the people we are to serve and protect and perpetrators are also carriers of different forms of energies. As such, one has to be very careful not to get sucked into the unhealthy vortex of chaos. Instead, you should seek to be the one to infect them with the positivity you carry in other for things not to escalate beyond your control so much that a form of brutal force may be required to set things in order.

For example, I never say what I feel like saying at any point in time. Instead, I speak what I have to say to get the job done. I try as much as possible to rehearse my speech and reaction because I know that one of my primary responsibilities is to control my energy and environment. It's almost as though I see it as my responsibility to suck you into my energy space, not the other way around; this does because it helps me a lot in de-escalating situations.

I believe so much in tactical language as I see it as a performing language that helps you become who you need to get the job done. I will be teaching you simple and practical ways to use these conversations in de-escalating situations.

Handling Insults and Abuse

According to statistics, the number one form of abuse is verbal abuse. People have many emotions stored up inside them and haven't mastered the art of being tactful when they speak. We have established that the most common language people use, the natural language, usually laden with raw emotions and hurts, causing more damage and hurting people's feelings than fixing it and towing the peace path.

One of the things that you need to understand, especially on the line of duty, is that insults are inevitable. A majority of the people you will come in contact with are either hurting or committed a crime. Most likely, they will have a preconceived notion about officers of the law.

What this innate predisposition does is that it somehow puts people on the defensive when talking to an officer because they feel we just might not get their perspective or probably we are always looking to find faults and puncture holes in stories to make it fit a suiting narrative that we are trying to bring up in our minds. Now, what usually happens as a result of this is that it triggers a predisposed response from people to us that might cause them to insult or verbally abuse you as an officer; and if not carefully taken, what was to be a simple conversation may quickly degenerate and escalate into a conversation nobody bargained for, and then there will be the use of force and unnecessary arrest.

Therefore, as law enforcement, you need to understand the art of tactical language, especially how to insulate yourself against verbal abuse and insult and learn how to de-escalate situations. The truth is most people don't know this, but they can have more control over conditions than they give themselves credit for if only they can learn to put in the requisite amount of work into it. What works most for de-escalating situations is the mastery of technical language, understanding, and awareness of self and your ability to assimilate and execute the art of de-escalation that I'm about to show you.

The first thing you need to know to do is the art of "Deflection."

A deflection is an act (and art) that deals with you, not allowing things to stick on you. Instead, as the word connotes, you deflect it off you more like letting things bounce off you rather than allowing it to stick on you like a gum. However, you must develop the kind of skin that bounces things off for you to do that.

THE HARDEST LANGUAGE

The truth is we were taught so many things growing up, and yes, life has also had its fair share in always trying to teach us things that are needed, but in all of this wealth of knowledge, no one prepared us how to act when we are insulted. People tell us to walk away from insults and not get sucked into unnecessary fights, more like avoiding fights by walking away. The problem with this is taking the challenge to walk away because it affects your esteem and makes you feel less of yourself, and sometimes it's about how it [walking away] makes other people perceive you as a weakling.

However, deflecting insults and verbal abuse is a more mature and better way to control conversations. It disempowers the perpetrators and gives you time to take control of the narrative. The art of deflection is so powerful. It's not about showing cowardice. Instead, it gives you the power and raises your energy level to the point where you are the one that infects and not the other way round.

To understand the art of deflection, the first thing you need to bear in mind is that everyone represents someone's ideology or an institution at every point in time. For example, as an officer of the law, you represent the law and the country; a salesman represents the product he's selling, and the list goes on. This understanding makes you know that there is a lot more at stake than you.

There is a way your organization or [the law/government] should respond to matters, and your response ought to be consistent with your superiors' response. If not, you are deemed disloyal and misaligned. If you do things your way all the time, you are only allowed to improve.

Steps to Note When De-escalating Situations

I like to think of de-escalating situations as an art rather than something to prevent unrest because, in my head, seeing it in light of the former makes it enjoyable for me, while seeing it as a preventive measure can somehow be agitating.

Now, to learn the art of de-escalating situations, I will share the practical steps you need to know and the techniques you will need to arm yourself.

a) **Don't allow yourself to be sucked into their negative vibe.** I have discovered that in as much as you shouldn't walk away from heated arguments or insults or situations, you also shouldn't allow yourself to be infected by it. Instead, learn to be in a position where you can effectively control the narrative. This strategy is done by understanding your frame of mind and having a healthy emotional quotient (as discussed in the previous chapter).

One way to do this is to psychologically maintain a close contact (not physically, as that may be confrontational). Close contact in the sense that you are not trying to back-off a conversation or distance yourself [your ideas, opinions, and possible reservations] from the subject matter. Instead, you are present and open to hearing the person out while actively maintaining your ground [which in this case is your composure, control, and balance]

b) Validate the other person's feelings with your words and actions [your non-verbal cues]. One of the mistakes people make when trying to de-escalate situations (or handling insults) is that they always want their opinions heard. Over time, it may degenerate to becoming a war of opinions, and when not managed properly, it escalates into something else.

However, one of the truths I have discovered about life is that everyone wants to be heard and valued. Also, everyone wants to know that the people that matter listen to them and are willing to consider their opinions and give it a try; even if it is not implemented, everyone is looking for empathy. Think about it this way. Most crimes and unrests happen because someone [or a set of people] wants to be heard; they want to be empowered. However, because most people aren't skilled in using tactical languages, they tend to let their emotions lead the way, which usually hurts [and expressions of hurt].

Your responsibility as a mature citizen [and an officer of the law] is to make people know that their opinion matters as well as heard by validating them through your words and actions without compromising the very establishment you represent.

Think about the recent uprising in the United States regarding the Black Lives Matter movement. You will discover that states with their police forces joining the movement enjoyed less violence and public defacing than those that had their police departments hold up barricades and went on a full riot-control mode.

I pointed all that out to make you see that when it comes to de-escalating situations, you have to be able to empathize with the person [perpetrator, group of people] and let them understand that you feel their pain. For example, you could say something like:

> "I might've done something worse if I were in your shoes, but..." or "I understand how you fee, but..."

What statements like that accomplish is that it makes the perpetrator feel like you understand him. It shows solidarity and opens him up to listen to whatever you have to say; however, it doesn't end there.

It is important to note that what you meant to validate is not the person's actions; instead, it is the person's feelings. The law does not punish or reward people for their feelings. Instead, people are held accountable for their actions; therefore, you should be careful when validating them. For example, a man murders another man because he sexually assaults a minor. Suppose I have a conversation with the perpetrator. In that case, I will understand his feelings. I will understand his anger and rage and disgust toward the other guy, but that doesn't necessarily mean that I should validate and empower murder.

c) Help the person find options. After you might have empathized and validated the person, the next thing to do is help them devise their calming down methods and not offer unsolicited solutions. Offering unsolicited solutions has the potential of re-escalating the situation, especially if you don't fully understand the problem in the first place.

For example, a White cop shouldn't tell an angry group of Black guys who have just gone through racial profiling's negatives that he understands how they feel. That will only infuriate them more.

Sometimes, in empathizing with people, most people make the mistake of equating their experiences with that of the person hurting; it's never the same. It may be similar situations and circumstances, but it is never the same experience because we see things differently, and our experiences are unique.

The most effective way to validate the person's feelings is to help them become aware of their actions and develop intentional ways to de-escalate the situation by assisting them to develop ways to solve the problems.

The truth is, when people are angry, they usually don't think. However, when they begin to calm, they are most likely prone to see the error in their ways and develop practical solutions to solve the problem they caused.

Another thing you can do is to, through design thinking, help them come up with practical ways to solve what's on the ground. You can ask questions like:

- "So, what do you think needs to be done now?"

- "How do you want to handle this?" "Do you think this is the best option?"

- "Would you like to take a moment to decide how best to handle this?"

When you do all this, what you are doing is that you are making them aware that they have control over how they feel, and as such, the consequences of their actions will be on them; either good or bad

d) Finally, respect their choice. Never make the mistake of imposing your opinion on someone agitated, as it has the potential of triggering more violent responses. The last thing you want to do is to make them pin the outcome of their anger on you.

THE HARDEST LANGUAGE

I jokingly tell people if you are tried for your crimes by the age of eighteen, it means that life expects you to be responsible for your actions. It's that simple. When you are de-escalating situations, you need to understand that people need to be accountable for their choices; and insomuch as you can, try to make sure that they make a right and safe choice. You have no power over what they do except it will hurt you or someone [or the community].

SUMMARY

1. There are two types of languages people use: natural and tactical Languages.

    a. Natural language is disastrous, and then it gives the need for tactical language.

    b. Tactical language is more of an intentional in its approach.

2. How to De-escalate Situations

    a. Don't allow yourself to be sucked into the vibe.

    b. Validate the other person's feelings.

    c. Help the person find options.

d. Respect their choice.

Chapter 3.

Processing the Information

The Secrets of Balanced Judgment

One of the most vital policing components has always been the ability to process vital information from what looks like little crumbs and weaving it like a master artisan to becoming an unbiased whole that can be reported and acted. Most of the time, the crumbs will always come to you as information via reports from victims, the community, eyewitnesses, and the likes.

People usually give reports in ways that exonerate them or prevent them from getting sucked into other people's businesses. This behavior is especially true in cases of eyewitness accounts. As such, it is natural for them to withhold information, sometimes very vital ones at that. Therefore, it is your responsibility to employ tactical questioning to dig out the real facts and not implied facts so you can be clear about the scenario.

Take, for example, you responded to a 911 call in the middle of the night, and upon arriving at the scene, you found a woman in a pool of blood, only that the blood isn't hers. It's her son's, who is wreathing in pain while cursing at his mom, and a teenage female is standing there shocked but unsurprised. From the look of things, it seems as though she's a family member too; complicated, right?

After de-escalating the situation and clearing the witnesses from the room, of course, with an ambulance arriving to take the injured fellow to the hospital for treatment, you will face the problem of questioning the witnesses and getting background information as to what happened. That is where the real work starts.

There are three kinds of people regarding questioning, and chances are you would've come in contact with at least two of them.

The first is the cooperative kind, who are usually incredibly open to questioning and will do all they can to help you have a balanced view of whatever is happening. It may be a question of motive, or this person is naturally cooperative and truthful to the authorities. It's always amazing to work with these people as they tend to make life easy for you, and you can quickly wrap up the questioning and get your facts right on time.

The second kind of person is what I call "Difficult People." It's always stressful working with them because it's hard to read them. They sometimes want to be that way. It may be wrong to lean toward saying that they are problematic because they are guilty; that will not be true. However, it may just be a disdain for talking to law enforcement officers, or they don't want to be a snitch of some sort, hence the need to uphold a "fictional" code.

And finally, we have the "Deceptive People." These can be nice to your face and even appear cooperative, only that they are not intentionally telling you the truth or would instead just send you on a wild goose chase. They are the ones who seem polite and appear like they give you a great vibe, only to report you and just shut down on you once they leave your presence. Perhaps their motive may be born from trying to stay on the fence and play on both sides of the divide; they are the type that won't go all-in during bets.

As a police officer, you will always contact these kinds of people in the line of duty; however, you may be doing yourself a disfavor by reacting to them based on what you sense them to be. Are you choosing to react to a difficult person with a show of force, or a cooperative person with open arms and warmth; or a deceptive person with a "carrot and stick" approach?

To be on top of your game and always control the situation, you will need to use tactical language. That way, you are aware of the situation, you can tailor the conversation, and you're always polite because you're always your best self. Understanding and mastering tactical languages are vital and can help you ask the right questions when processing the information available to you.

So, having understood these three kinds of people and establishing that the most basic and effective way to communicate and get valid information out of them is through the use of tactical language, the big question then becomes, "How do you generate compliance amongst people?

How to Generate Compliance from People

According to the Verbal Judo Institute, founded by George Doc Thompson, there are five critical tools you need to have to generate compliance from anyone and win them over to your side by getting them to talk. The Institute coined an acronym for it – LEAPS, and it stands for **L**isten, **E**mpathize, **A**sk, **P**araphrase, and **S**ummarize.

L – *Listening*

According to George Thompson, most people would naturally say that the opposite of speaking is listening, but that's not true; he says the opposite is more like "waiting," and I very much agree with that. There is usually someone waiting to talk back at the other end of a conversation rather than listening. It's almost as though everyone is trying to air their opinion and stop at nothing to be heard, even if it means losing vital information that someone else may be saying at that moment. What we don't know is listening plays a very crucial role.

You need to understand that tactical listening happens to be the first step in generating compliance rather than waiting. It has nothing to do with being a cop or not; instead, this is a skill that is very vital for everyday life. The reason is that most times when people talk, they often tell you what the problem is [that they are not saying] and also give you perspectives that you may never have had before. Additionally, most people tend to like to be treated a certain way and drop clues on how they want to, as well, and all these happen to give you vital information and help broaden your horizon and get more perspective.

For you to master the art of tactical listening, there are four things you must do:

1. **Be open and unbiased**. You shouldn't enter a conversation with a preconceived notion; people can smell that. Instead, you need to be able to ignore whatever fact (or truth) you think you have and be open-minded when a person is talking to you. That will give you leverage because people can smell if you understand them, are willing to understand them, or you have a bias against them.

2. **Hear literally**. This is a tricky one. Never attach a meaning to something or infer what you think is said. It's always best to hear things how it is being said rather than how you want to hear it. Again, hearing the way you wish to alludes to the fact that you have a preconceived notion, which will always alter your sense of sound judgment and repels the person to whom you are speaking. So, it is safe to say that you hear people literally at all times.

3. **Interpret accurately.** It's always nice to understand what people say and interpret their intended meaning, and if it is not clear, you tactically ask questions. For example, you may want to interject and clarify by saying, "Is this what you really mean?" Or, make statements like, "Help me understand a little, can I say that this is

what you meant?" What this does is that it makes the person know that you are following and may make them divulge more information.

4. **Act Appropriately.** This deals with your response and reaction to the shared information. Bear in mind that an adverse reaction may cause the person to withhold more information from you, while a positive one may get them to be safer around you.

E – Empathize

Nothing communicates support and openness like being empathetic toward people when they speak, especially bearing in mind that most people believe you to be the representative of the institution you represent – either the government or the product you're selling; or an office you're occupying.

The truth is employing the process of empathetic communication happens to be one of the most effective ways that people know that you understand them – and you have to do a whole lot of that. Now, most times, people tend to confuse empathy for sympathy; they are both different. Think of it this way:

Sympathy is more about absorbing the feeling of sorrow and guilt another person [or a group of people] face. You personalize the feeling and make it your reality, while empathy is about understanding others' feelings, not absorbing the feeling. As an empath, you will understand why they did what they had to do, but then you're not emotionally attached to the person who made a choice [or decision]. Sympathy comes with a high level of emotional attachment that may be detrimental, while empathy is more focused and goal-oriented.

As a law enforcement officer, you should be able to empathize and not sympathize with people, so your sense of judgment isn't clouded by one narrative at the expense of the collective or the community. The best way to define empathy is into three states:

1. The way you interpret the problem deals with the information you generated before engaging the person in a conversation and open dialogue.

2. The way you see the problem from their viewpoint validates the person's feelings and point of view.

3. The way you see their problem through your eyes; is the peak of empathy as it opens you up to a world of understanding about the case at hand.

A – Ask Questions

I can boldly tell you that nothing looks like what it seems at first glance. Therefore, it is your responsibility to find out the truth by asking the right questions at the right time – and under the proper condition.

It's so good that you ask for clarification whenever you are not clear so that you don't jump to false conclusions. One of the most effective methods I know [and has proven well over the years] is the concept of design thinking. Design thinking is a way of asking intelligent and leading questions to come up with customer-focused answers.

Now in asking questions, you don't want to be confrontational. Preferably you want the person you're talking with to settle into the idea of you and trust that you are their best interest at heart. Therefore, it is advisable to form a bond (or a relationship) with them through listening and empathizing. You begin to ask the right questions.

There are five (5) basic questions that you want to ask at this point:

1. **Fact-finding Questions** - These questions are for seeking clarity based on available facts. For example, "Where were you when it happened?" Or use it to cross-reference already known facts.

2. **Leading Questions -** These questions help you connect dots and seek to open up more details, especially if you are well informed about the narrative. Leading questions help you root out what people don't want to say, but you know it exists.

3. **Opinion-seeking Questions** - These questions are not about inditing anyone; instead, they are directed at knowing what the person thinks based on perceived expertise, hoping that there can be some recommendations regarding the subject matter.

4. **Direct Questions** - These sorts of questions are all about going straight to the point to find out missing pieces; and

5. **General Questions** - You should note that a series of wrong questions may cause the person to spiral out of control, and it may be hard for you to get the kind of assistance and openness you want.

P – Paraphrase

The concept of paraphrasing is all about repeating what was said back to the person to ensure that you get the right message, and you understand what was said. Earlier in the opening chapter, I posited that communication isn't complete until the receiver has understood the message. He gives feedback; well, that's true even for the person engaging in tactical listening, which I assume is you.

You must paraphrase what is being said [in your own words] and confirm from the person if you are interpreting what he is communicating well. Most times, what people give are bits and pieces of information, but you will then have to pull all the pieces together to make it whole and repeat it back to them for clarity.

S – Summarize

The concept of a summary is all about brevity and taking it steps to be clear and concise in your communication. You will have to make decisions in split seconds. Let them know that whatever you say can be assumed that the organization you represent says it because it will be perceived that way.

One thing to understand about conversational dynamics is that you need to make a reasonable allowance for interjections during conversations. These interjections can often throw you off balance and send you on another tangent. Therefore, you must stay on point and address every interjection when communicating it.

For example, you may be talking about something, and then the person you're interviewing interjects and raises an opinion. After you tactically listened to the person, you should deem it fit to take them back to the compelling points of the conversation you're having; you reinforce your stance on the matter. You may want to say something like, "Thank you for this. Is there anything else you would like to add?"

The conversation will continue as long as you keep listening.

Another thing that you now need to be sure of is that you will need to take feedback to be sure they know you understood them. Also, be aware of your decisions and why you had to make them.

SUMMARY

1. There are three kinds of people you will encounter when it comes to processing information and during a questioning session:

    a. Cooperative People

    b. Deceptive People

    c. Difficult people.

    The only way to deal with these people in a unified way is to use tactical language and tactical listening.

2. To generate compliance, you will need to employ the LEAPS toolkit. LEAPS is an acronym for:

   L – Listening
   E – Empathize
   A – Ask Questions
   P – Paraphrase
   S – Summarize

Chapter 4.

Police Force and Police Shootings

It's hard to look at the current events around us and not get aggrieved by the fact that police shootings exist in our communities, and with the rate at which it is escalating and causing a lot of civil unrest, I believe is it time to speak up about it.

According to statistics provided by *The Washington Post*, one thousand people have been killed by the police force between June 2019 and June 2020, and a more alarming statistic is that the number has been steady since 2015.

An excerpt on *The Washington Post* website reads:

> *After Michael Brown, an unarmed black man, was killed in 2014 by police in Ferguson, Mo., a Post investigation found that the FBI undercounted fatal police shootings by more than half. This is because reporting by police departments is voluntary, and many departments fail to do so.*
>
> *The Post's data relies primarily on news accounts, social media postings, and police reports. Analysis of more than five years of data reveals that the number and circumstances of fatal shootings and the victims' overall demographics have remained relatively constant.*

A further study of these shootings and violent patterns shows that the rate of police killings isn't racially motivated, especially when considered in the number of people across the United States. However, the case becomes different. The data shows otherwise when we consider the killings in light of racial spread, especially considering the total population of Blacks, Hispanics, and Whites across the United States.

"Although half of the people shot and killed by police are White, Black Americans are shot at a disproportionate rate. They account for less than 13 percent of the U.S. population, but are killed by police at more than twice the rate of white Americans. Hispanic Americans are also killed by police at a disproportionate rate." **The Washington Post**

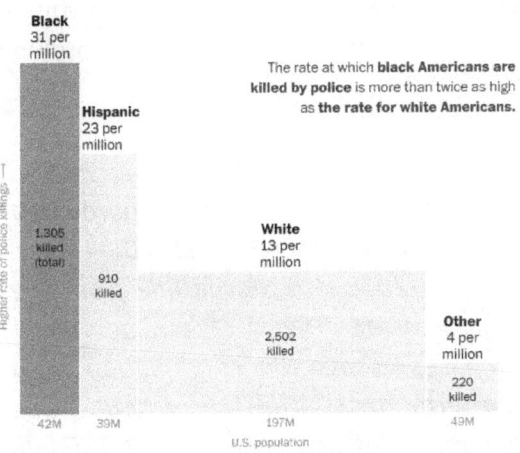

When you understand these statistics, one may be able to justify the Black Lives Matter movement. Then, some would want to say that "All lives matter," because if the information is looked at from the viewpoint of the number of people killed, one may be tempted to say that we should move past racial divides and politics and address the issue of police violence that's plaguing our beautiful land of freedom and hope.

Another fact to note is that there's no state where Police shooting hasn't occurred across the United States in this time period, and it has always affected more young people (especially males) than older people. The states with the highest rate of shootings are New Mexico, Alaska, and Oklahoma.

But then, do these statistics paint the whole picture?

A factor that may have influenced this statistic may also be the country's reality of crime rates. According to *USA Today*:

> *"There were more than 1.2 million incidents of rape, robbery, aggravated assault, and murder reported in the United States in 2018 – a 3% decline from the previous year. The decrease in violent crime represents the continuation of a long-term trend. The U.S. violent crime rate stands at 381 incidents per 100,000 people, down from a high of 758 per 100,000 in 1991."*

> *However, crime is a local phenomenon, and in some states, violent crime rates are nearly as high or higher than they were nationwide in the early 1990s. Using data*

from the FBI's 2018 Uniform Crime Reporting Program, 24/7 Wall St. reviewed statewide violent crime rates to identify the most dangerous states in America. We ranked all states and listed them from the lowest violent crime rate to the highest.

Violent crime in the United States is most likely to be committed in urban areas. Even in many of the country's safest states, there are cities with violent crime rates that exceed the national average by a wide margin. Similarly, it is no coincidence that many of the states with the highest violence rates are also home to some of America's most dangerous cities. In some cases, a single city can account for over one-quarter of all violent crime in an entire state.

The question then is, "Do all these justify Police shootings across the country?" The answer is no.

Although it seems to be a general perception that most of the issues that arose with police shootings are racially motivated and that in itself is a matter that carries so much weight due to its sensitivity, and thanks to the media who may want to politicize this, it is always better to understand the truth from a holistic perspective to give a balanced judgment and deal with the root cause issue.

In my opinion, I don't see the shootings as a problem. Instead, I think that we are losing our moral code as a country and that in itself is alarming. A holistic approach will mean that we also consider the number of officers who have been killed or wounded in the line of duty and extrapolate the data against the number of police officers we have.

I am going to quote an article written by Nial McCarthy posted on the *Forbes* website:

> *"The FBI has released its latest statistics regarding line-of-duty deaths and/or assaults on law enforcement officers in the United States. A total of 106 police officers lost their lives on duty last year, a 13% increase in 2017. 55 officers were feloniously killed while 51 died accidentally. The average age of officers killed feloniously was 37, and they had an average tenure of 10 years in law enforcement. Three were female, and 52 were male.*
>
> *When it comes to the circumstances behind non-accidental deaths, 23 officers were killed in the course of investigative or*

enforcement activities. Another 11 lost their lives in ambushes while six died in pursuits. Line-of-duty deaths occurred in 28 states and Puerto Rico. Out of all states, Georgia had the highest number of police officer deaths in 2018 with five, followed by Florida and California, with four each. 55 of the officers who died in 2018 were killed with firearms."

And below is the infographic chat for these statistics.

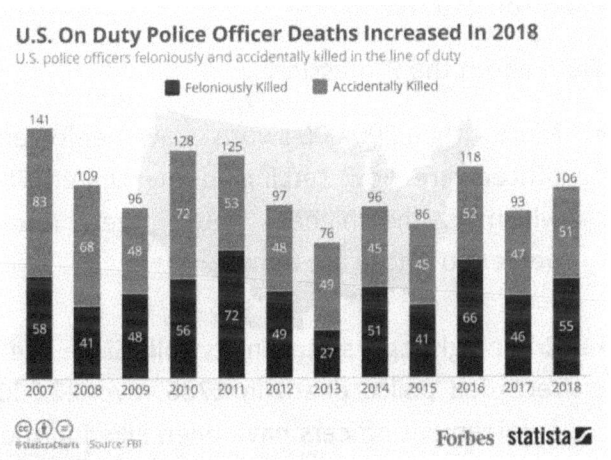

THE HARDEST LANGUAGE

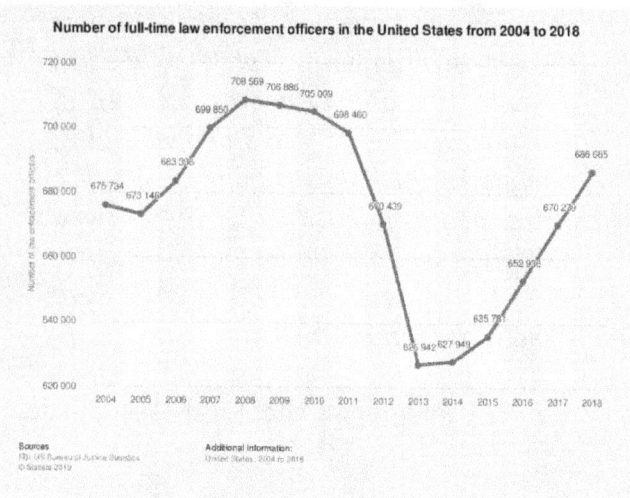

Now according to NLE

Key Data about the Profession

- More than 800,000 sworn law enforcement officers are now serving in the United States, which is the highest figure ever. About **12 percent** of those are female.

- Crime-fighting has taken its toll. Since the first recorded police death in 1786, over 22,000 law enforcement officers have been killed in the line of duty. Currently, there are **22,217** names engraved on the walls of the National Law Enforcement Officers Memorial.

- A total of **1,627** law enforcement officers died in the line of duty during the past ten years, an average of one death every **54** hours or **163** per year. There were **135** law enforcement officers killed in the line of duty in 2019.

- According to the FBI's *Uniform Crime Report,* 2018 LEOKA report: There have been **58,866** assaults against law enforcement officers in 2018, resulting in **18,005** injuries.

- The **1920s** were the deadliest decade in law enforcement history, when a total of **2,517** officers died, or an average of almost **252** each year. In **1930, 312** officers died in the line of duty, making it the deadliest year in law enforcement history. That figure dropped dramatically in the **1990s** to an average of **163** per year.

- In law enforcement history, the deadliest day was September 11, 2001, when **72** officers were killed while responding to America's terrorist attacks.

- The New York City Police Department has lost more officers in the line of duty than any other department, with **941** deaths. Texas has lost **1,772** officers, more than any other state. The state with the fewest deaths is Vermont, with **24**.

- There are **1,181** federal officers listed on the Memorial and **720** correctional officers, and **44** military law enforcement officers.

- There are **365** female officers listed on the Memorial; **11** female officers were killed in 2019.

I am trying to say that both sides have known a significant number of losses, and the solution isn't an increased level of bigotry and hatred (or apprehension) as the case may be. You have the average law enforcement officer in a high-crime area always on edge – especially those assigned to homicide and narcotics because they fear that they may get back to their families injured.

I am not saying that any of these factors are not motivated by racial hatred, killings, and other atrocities against humanity, because that's how I see it, in all honesty. Instead, what I am saying is that it is easier to see from your standpoint than it is to see holistically. Most times, seeing things in a broader view helps your understanding of the situation and makes you know that there's a lot that needs to be put in place for change to happen.

You wouldn't blame an average person who grew up in the streets or the slums and all he knows is thug-life and drugs; whose orientation while growing up has been to see the police as an enemy or a threat to his success, or a Black [or Hispanic] guy who has been programmed to know the stings of racism and see white police officers as the enemy who might be looking for all means to harass and mistreat him. Of course, on the other side of the divide is an officer who has heard so much about the extremes and mentally positioned to see his firearm as his only form of protection from the harm that the community poses. I have come across a few law-enforcement officers who feel as though the law is for saner people, and a whole lot of people [in our communities] don't fall into that category. As such, they feel the law is powerless to protect them as individuals. At one time, someone once said to me that he isn't ready to be a part of people's statistics hurt on duty, so rather than taking the coward's way of quitting, he'd rather trust his legal firearm to do the protecting. All these and more contribute to the ever-increasing tension we face as a community.

Do People Take Advantage of Police Officers?

Well, this is a million-dollar question that may seem to have an obvious answer, but when studied holistically, you will find out that there's more to it.

Hollywood and other media channels may have succeeded and painting narratives in people's minds; some great and others not-so-great. However, one will be naïve to think that there aren't situations where people take advantage of some officers – not all.

A civilian once said to me that the rich and affluent have a way of buying over police officers for their cause – something he calls systemic corruption, while the police trample and intimidates those who are weaker.

The truth is, I don't believe this statement to be an accurate representation of the police force because that would be insulting to the good people who have served with their blood promoting peace. It would also mean dishonoring the countless lives lost due to gun violence and gang wars.

Law enforcement is an institution governed by statutes and principles with the primary objective of upholding the law within a sovereign state and community. Some individuals are enrolled to help enforce this standard, and these individuals represent the institution to the people. However, people need to note that the individuals [who have their own wills and rights] are not more prominent than the institution. One individuals' actions should not represent the whole [institution].

Yes, there are good cops and not-so-good cops; however, we shouldn't define an institution based on individual morality. Hence there will be no need for binding statutes and laws. Ensuring that those who falter within the system are held accountable for their actions, and sometimes at higher standards than civilians. Those who perform exceptionally well are rewarded and recognized in the system and the community at large.

Around April 2020, I watched how people expected the police to arrest those causing public unrest during the nationwide protests, and I laughed so hard.

A guy went to rob and store, and fortunately, as he stepped out, an officer was there who had his weapon drawn and shouted, "Freeze!" The robber then raised one hand and began to shout that he'll comply, all the while walking to his car. Meanwhile, the officer just kept on screaming, "Don't move," but the guy didn't listen. That episode continued until the robber got to his car, picked up his gun, and pointed it at the officer, who then had to put his hands up and watched the robber sped off.

As comical as that sounds, I bet that it represents how people expect the police to treat those they are about to arrest. I believe in treating people with the utmost respect and dignity. Trust me; I know that it can be challenging to do so at times. Still, you cannot sacrifice the work that needs to be done on the altar of respect; instead, you should be intelligent enough to infuse respect and leverage on the intelligence that comes with it to execute your duties well without resorting to force and violence.

Looking at the situation holistically, I think the problem is we expect too much from each other, both the police and the citizens. Is it possible that we feel entitled and as though either of our realities are superior to the other? The community sees law enforcement officers as those who are to serve and always maintain peace. They hold them accountable to treat people with respect, irrespective of the situation, or the offense.

Law enforcement expects people to always be on their best behavior. They expect people to know the law and intentionally abide by it. However, it doesn't always work that way.

SUMMARY

Police shootings aren't necessarily a function of racial injustice but reveal a more resounding crack that can only mend and heal when both parties (police and civilians) take responsibility to build a better society.

Chapter 5

Talk to Me

Contrary to many popular opinions most cops have about how civilians see us, we [men in blue] are undervalued and can be trampled upon; that is not necessarily true. Many people value our profession and do not see us as a group of people that need pity; instead, as faithful citizens who will stop at nothing to ensure that there are peace and security in our environment.

You may want to elude this perception to the media (especially the movie industry) who have helped in immeasurable ways to paint us as effective, efficient, respectful, and always dutiful and sacrificial – with no flaws and a fantastic response-time when it comes to being called upon; which is an excellent representation of us by the way, however, we need to understand that we can by ourselves tear down that incredible work they have tried to build for us [I meant Hollywood!]

However, it is also possible to tear this construct down in reality by ourselves simply because we lack the requisite skills to communicate effectively and be open enough for people to approach us and be friends with us. Most times, we tend to respond with the natural language [which is always uncouth] and is often a reflection of the hurts and stress we face emotionally and on the job.

However, sometimes we need to pause and intentionally work on us being approachable. You never can tell how much that can help you have a smooth day, especially with the people in your community.

For example, I have seen situations where an officer required rescuing from being lynched by the people in the neighborhood who he's been kind to over the years. He [the officer] happened to be a friendly guy in the hood, and a lot of the locals knew him and identified with him; then, one day, he found himself amid an altercation between two rival gang parties. Being the only one on the scene, he felt he could mediate, but things soon escalated, and the gang members were about to lynch him. His saving grace was that a few people in the hood knew him and were very ready to step in – which they did.

I've also seen several other cases of people coming to [an] officers' rescue and other cases where civilians have interfered with making an arrest go easy. For example, I know an officer who once had a violent altercation during an arrest. It was so dramatic that the assailant threw him on his back, landed some jibes, and was about running off till the people around had to round him up and put him down. It was so bad that a civilian took the cuffs off the officer to use on him [the assailant].

I think it will be unfair to say that the general perception people have toward the police officer is usually that of hostility and apprehension; on the contrary, I think some respect us and will do anything to comply with us and make our day go smooth; however, to increase the perception for people to see us in a positive light, we need to collectively and individually take responsibility for how we paint ourselves to them and make them feel warm, welcome and open around us.

In this chapter, I will be talking deeply about how to be open and inviting when talking to people in such a way that those who come in contact with you feel as though you help lift a burden off their shoulder, not that you added more to what was causing an excruciating pain [and racial divide].

I will also be amplifying the immeasurable values of effective communications [and avoid niceties] by giving real-life examples of officers who have practical and tactical communication to be better people and even had amazing days on and off the field. I will see these values and give you a psychological reason to adopt this line of thinking.

(Make no mistake, it does not come easy and requires consistent practice to achieve the best result and master the art of having the hard [yet] simple conversations.

THE HARDEST LANGUAGE

I will not deny that a few people dread officers of the law and will stop at nothing to avoid a confrontation or even something as harmless as an interview or questioning – even if you guaranty them anonymity, talk more of when you try to assure them that will have the full backing of the law. (Well, in their defense, sometimes it is hard to believe that 'good' will always have your back, especially when the fear of likely repercussions from the community [or individuals, gangs, associations], and this has a psychological effect on people level of cooperation with law enforcement).

However, the onus still lies on [the police community] to make people safe and feel at peace by understanding that the law is always behind those who are righteous according to its standards and that we [as individuals who represents the law] are approachable and always seeking to help by having a warm demeanor and countenance at every point in time.

The Magic of Opening people up to you!

Somehow [for reasons beyond what most of us will know] there's always a form of apprehension people have when talking to the police. Well, it may not be great to say it in absolute terms; a fairer way would be to say that people usually have a predisposition about having conversations with a law enforcement officer – for some, it may be a little bit of apprehension, while for others, it may be with an air of superiority; while for yet another set of people, it may be a friendly or neutral tone - - whichever one it is, usually it is determined by the wealth of information they have had about officers of the law or things that they have seen or heard by the people in their communities and spheres.

However, irrespective of how a civilian is approaching you, you can by yourself determine how you want people to feel around you without compromising on the quality of policing you dish out based on sentiments and other narratives that may want to pressure you to give an imbalanced viewpoint.

To attain this, the first thing you need to do is ensure you have the right energy around you. Believe it or not, we wear a demeanor that either attracts people to us or repels them. Most people often feel as though it is by happenstance that people [police and civilians alike] will open up and begin to divulge critical information or cooperate with questioning; however, it is not so.

More has to do with the person's demeanor initiating the conversation, and in a weird scientific way, this is usually so.

Usually, the first thing determining factor is premised on the look and feel. As an officer of the law, how do you look? Intimidating or inviting? Rough or warm? There is a reason why in the corporate world, most people prefer smart women to represent their brands and close deals, especially in a male-dominated environment because somehow, men become more relaxed and open when they see [smart and intelligent] women – for some odd reasons, we usually keep our guards down around them. (If you don't believe me, begin to note how protective and open you get around your daughters – if you're a dad – or your sisters; and if you're an all-boys family, you may have been wondering why people get protective of their female family members). You need to understand that people are either drawn to us or repelled by the energy we disseminate right from within us.

THE HARDEST LANGUAGE

The second determinant is how you make people feel when they are around you. Your ability to project and communicate warmth and welcome while not compromising the quality of the policing you do or bending to the whims of anyone is vital. You need to learn the subtle art of making people feel very comfortable around you, so much so that they will begin to divulge what they deem to be sensitive information without being forced and coerced.

Some will not comply, but you do not have to let that deter you at all – especially as you begin the journey. However, I can assure you that as you continue and practice this over time, you will get the hang of it, and it will become more effortless and seamless.

You can start by practicing something as simple as responding politely to civilians asking for direction at your duty post or keeping people back at a crime scene.

For example, a man can walk up to you and ask for the direction to a mall around, and instead of being warm and polite, you say something like: "The mall is just down the corner, keep walking you will get there," and you say it in the meanest of tone possible, while not even looking at the person to establish eye contact. I am sure that such a person will feel undervalued and wonder why their taxes pay to take care of you.

Another approach, however, can be this: Same scenario, however, rather than turning the person off with your comment, you say something like:

"Oh, a great afternoon to you! The mall is just a few blocks away from you by the corner. But you know what? If you don't get the description, here's my number, you can call me to inform me where you are, and I'll direct you," or you can say something like: "If you miss the turn or get confused, I'll be right here."

Take a second and assume you are the individual. How do you think the second response will make you feel? That warmth, welcome, and excitement will sure get anyone and would go a long way in helping people feel so respected and loved to be around you – now that's an excellent score for the Police department.

The truth is we represent not just our police department. Still, the law and the government and thinking about the many frustrations that most people may have with the establishment (the government) at the moment, we need to learn to be a friendly face at every point in time. You know what most people forget is that we are humans too; humans who are entitled to their opinions and have emotions too – and what this means is that it's not every time that we as individuals agree [or are in accordance] with the government and some policies too. However, we must learn to lay aside our biases and respectfully [and dare I add diligently] carry out the job required of us; showing and amplifying the good side all the time; not as often as possible!

Another reason for being big on the idea of warmth and welcome is the fact that you should try as much as possible not to let people leave your presence with a negative intention and experience – it is critical. We are paid with their hard-earned

THE HARDEST LANGUAGE

dollar (that is a way to look at it). As such, we owe them a responsibility to be just and fair at all times – especially in our engagement with them.

This does not mean that people should be baby-seated or indulged in any way; instead, it is a call to be more professional and intentional when on the line of duty and during interactions.

Another example can be when processing people at the precinct. You have to take their statements, get their mugshots, and detain them [and do all necessary detaining processes]. I'm sure this is a situation with which most of us are familiar. Honestly, the room's energy during this process – I'm talking about the people's energy – is never a positive one. Dare I say that ninety-five percent of the time, you have people feeling grumpy, pained, angered and whatever negative emotions that come with being caught in an act that disrupts public peace, or [sometimes] wrongfully accused and other unfortunate things that might have transpired outside.

Now because of the concentration of negative energy, I can imagine that it will be hard to remain calm and professional through and through, such that even if you plan to be calm and professional before your shift starts, chances are two to three hours into your shift, it may begin to rub off on you. You feel the urge to mirror the responses you're getting – especially if an alcoholic [who still has a modicum of consciousness and is brash] – but it doesn't have to be like that.

You must understand that you are solely responsible for the energy you disseminate and your heart's protection to ensure that you do not take in some negativity with you. So, for example, rather than responding brashly to the people brought in for processing, you can say something like:

"Excuse me, will you please cooperate and let me do my job so I can get you out of here real fast?" When you say something like this respectfully, what you are communicating is that you still value the person irrespective of the situation and that you are not judgmental. You may even ask what happened and then ask if the person wants to reach out to anyone.

When done right, all this will go a long way in ensuring that the person is calm and even influence their energy level by elevating it to meet yours. You need to understand that matching negative energy with negative responses is you stooping low to a level that is way below the office you represent – and you can't afford to do that.

You need to understand that one of the most basic human needs is acknowledging and respecting. At all times, you need to learn to accord people these two [without compromising] regardless of who they are, where they come from, or what race they belong to; and this isn't just about policing; it also spills into every other walk of life – it is a principle.

(Principles are universal, and as such, will work in any part of the world and any industry, while laws vary and are determined by the conditions set between a boundary).

Now, here is the real deal: You cannot give what you do not have, meaning that you cannot respect people if you do not respect yourself as a person first. You cannot be treating yourself like trash and expect to treat someone else better – it just does not work that way. You need to intentionally take care of yourself and practice these things first with yourself (especially when you fall short of your standards); then, with your household members, after which you can try it on your colleagues and then the people around you.

Chapter 6.

Understanding and Practicing Non-Verbal Cues

I know it is possible to see the task of implementing all these ideas as daunting and sometimes impractical, but I want to assure you that is not the case. On the contrary, I believe it's even easier to do, and all it takes is the willingness to commit to doing what is needed and reframing your mind, as this will help you put in the necessary work.

I will not promise you that there won't be major setbacks at first or you even reverting to old ways of doing things; trust me, it will most definitely happen. However, as I said in previous chapters, you get better at the craft over time.

THE HARDEST LANGUAGE

I have had times where I flaunted this ideology. I'll say that it has happened several times, seeing that I had a "street background." I was born in the street, rolled in the street, got fed by the street, and went through numerous hustles and hassles, moving from home to home. Then I went on to sign up for the military, where things are gruesome, and a measure of ruggedness is needed – but that is no excuse.

Being a Police officer [or a Po-Po, as the street calls us] comes with a different level of responsibility and requirement – one that demands that you become a mixture of a rugged gangster and a caring mother. These requirements and mixture will demand something from you because the neighborhood's peace rests on your shoulders and that of your colleagues.

Now due to this reality, in this chapter, I will be giving you a lot of insights into the science of non-verbal communications and give a detailed description of various cues and how to interpret them and use them to your advantage, especially when interviewing people. There will be times when you misread and misinterpret cues, but that is nothing to worry about as you will get better at it.

Now I feel the need to stress this next statement strongly:

You should not; under any circumstance, make any final decisions and conclusions based on a hunch or the need to get over a case very fast because you believe that you are a good judge of character or fully mastered the art of reading non-verbals. There is a reason why the system is big on proofs and pieces of evidence that can be substantiated. What

understanding this science does is that it helps you probe further and improves your investigative prowess.

The Science behind Non-Verbals

We do not just communicate via the words we speak **when** we have conversations with people. Instead, the energy we carry inside of us at every moment becomes a driving force and gets us to begin to act in particular [universal] ways that communicate our most authentic feelings. You could also get a whole series of clues about lies, deception, and truthfulness; you can get millions of reactions and interpretations of a person's true nature and intentions just by understanding non-verbals. Simply put, non-verbals are anything that communicates but is not a word.

How we dress and how we walk have meanings, and we use that to interpret what is in the minds of the people around us and even go steps further to employ it in determining friends or foe; those who are open to our company those who are not.

The truth is that there is an uncanny and reflex-based way of us, basing our security on the concept of non-verbal communications. Oddly, someone will come to you and tell you that he wants to harm you, right? Instead, what you notice, react or respond to [in a bid to feel safe] is the person's body language; how the person paces around you; your insecurity at the ATM at night or when you're walking through a dark alley, and there's no one around; or when you tell someone to hands-up, and he's trying to reach into the jacket while looking "suspicious" – we all do it; as a matter of fact, most of us select our mates based on non-verbals.

THE HARDEST LANGUAGE

We may feel we are very sophisticated and can keep a calm composure without giving off anything. Still, we are never in a state where we are not transmitting information – as long as your mind is active and you're processing a thought, your body will always dance to the tune of the information you're processing and react accordingly.

MYTHS ABOUT NON-VERBALS

There are many myths out there on the clues that we give regarding non-verbals, especially seeing many movies that talked about some of the signs and gestures, and they are wrong.

So, let's hold up a little: I still wouldn't get why people would feel like movies will divulge so much real information to the detriment of National Security and expose special trade secrets!

In the section, I will be sharing some of the posture and position myths that go around about body language and what those postures really mean.

1. **Folded arms.** People generally believe that when you are talking to someone whose arms are folded, it usually means that the person is trying to block off or withhold critical information; well, that's not true.

The folded arm posture is a posture people take for self-soothing. It makes people comfortable in themselves and sometimes may mean they are settling into the conversation, and it is done more in public than in private.

2. **Looking the other way.** This is usually a misconception people have when you have a conversation with someone, and then the person tries looking the other way. Looking around is usually tagged as an act of deception or avoidance – after all, people should not have to think too hard when telling the truth, right? Well, that is not always true!

Looking the other way can indicate someone trying to think through or process something, and the truth is, it is only natural to process information before giving it out.

3. **Stuttering and fidgeting.** Most people feel that when someone's words are not clear, it is an indicator of deception or withholding information – probably because the person has to think on his [or her] feet. The basis for this argument is that those who have nothing to hide usually have nothing to fear.

Well, I'm afraid that's not right. I have seen people who are innocent stutter so much that when they begin to recount information, they will look as though they are the guilty one; meanwhile, it could just be that they are tired or in shock and unsettled at that point. Some people do not even process things fast and only remember details over time or when they feel a little bit relaxed.

4. **Throat clearing; touching of nose and Covering of mouth.** Another misconception is that when people do any of these three things [touching of the nose, covering of the mouth, and throat clearing], they are lying and have something to hide, and as such, they are not straight – well, this isn't true either.

These behaviors are also self-soothers, and people do them when they want to get comfortable or are uneasy, not necessarily with the situation or with the questioning or conversation. Instead, they may feel uneasy with their body system and may need to be calm. Sometimes, they may also be processing information (especially the nose touching; it's not weird).

One of the things I have come to discover about these things [while studying] is that people tend to make a lot of personality projection when interpreting body language. Also, there might be a tendency to want to project your hunch on someone by validating them [these hunches] with the behavioral pattern of the person you're questioning.

While following your hunch is great and is always a useful tool when interacting with people, you must also learn to stay with the fact (as much as you can gather) and process them based on your data. I tell people this: "let your hunch always be in the confines of the facts and shreds of evidence you have – that's where genuine professionalism comes in.

BODY LANGUAGES AND THE SUBCONSCIOUS

Many of us are familiar with the concept of computer programming - maybe not in the context of coding programming languages - but in the light of updating our system's software for optimal productivity, better performance, or up-to-date upgrades. The truth is most times when we are notified to install these updates, no matter how inconvenient it feels at that moment, chances are we tend to always click on it.

The updates are so integral and essential to our user experience that even when we don't click to install it, over time, the system will self-install as long as it remains connected to the internet.

In the same vein, we have our programming software that dictates how we behave and how we feel about things happening around us. Still, it also dictates how we respond to them by eliciting different behavioral patterns and responses that make up the entire body language spectrum.

Our mind's subconscious cortex has been found to process over 40 million pieces of information per second and then instruct us to pick and react efficiently. A common example is rooted in how we fold our arms or interlock our fingers between each other.

If you observe closely, you will see that there's a certain way you fold your hands – a particular pattern you employ when you do so, and it is almost as though it is instinctive. The same goes for how you interlock your fingers; these things are patterns that functions as programming from the subconscious mind, so much so that when you try to alter the programming, you will find yourself struggling within yourself and questioning when you have to do it that way in the first place.

For example, change the positioning of your arms when you fold them, and you will see that there will be a struggle in the form of uneasiness and awkwardness. The same goes for interlocking your fingers – that might even make the discomfort worse.

This phenomenon is referred to as Cognitive Dissonance in psychology. It is defined as what happens when you decide to consciously change a specific pattern and habit that you have always known to be your norm – and everyone goes through it when they decide to institute a change in themselves.

However, the mechanism is such that you cannot affect a change [in habit or behavioral pattern] without intentionally reconstructing your subconscious's programming, and it doesn't take much. It just takes consistency on your part. I believe it is the path to upgrade our programming and better understand our body languages (our non-verbal cues).

You may be wondering why this is important, but the truth is that in dealing with people, most times, we tend to discount the words we hear for the things that we see, and yes, the subconscious runs the majority of our body language. As such, as officers of the law, we need to understand how to manage ourselves and give off the right energy, and at the same time be able to accurately interpret the energy that people give off in other to make us better understand them and see beyond what they are saying [and how they act].

Your behavioral pattern defines your Outcome in life

One of the things that we need to understand is that success and failure are a cumulation of behavioral patterns that we exhibit at every point in time, and as such, the need to focus on it can never be wrong. You may be wondering how that affects you (or policing) and here is how.

The strength of the character we exhibit per time is dependent on how we feel. For example, If I feel weak, I will use weak body language, and when I feel strong, I will exhibit the same, and my actions will also reflect that - Success has a behavioral pattern.

A person who feels weak, for example, will exhibit weak postures like slouching, entering into his or her shell, and display characteristics of being timid – for example, leaning too much on one leg. In contrast, a person who has a strong mental structure will stand upright and even have a look that's commanding. Ever heard the phrase: "You're addressed the way you dress?" Well, it is so true.

To better understand this, one needs to look at the concept of gravity, that earth's downward pull on everything, and yes. At the same time, it keeps our feet firmly planted on the ground, so we don't float away into space. It also has a way of pulling our bodies into a slouching posture because **Gravity pulls down on us consistently.** However, we need to get to a point where we understand that gravity's downward pull can also weigh on our emotional and psychological responses and life disposition.

You are not your best when you slouch and look weak. You will be surprised that just by changing your posture and standing up straight tends to increase your productivity astronomically and communicate confidence to people around you.

Three Major kinds of people based on body language dynamics

Now, this section is not about being absolute because most times, you find one person exhibiting more than one of these three traits; however, what I am giving here is what to look out for, first in yourself, and then in people so that you can know how to evaluate yourself better, the people you come in contact with and then deal with them accordingly.

1. **The Lookers**. These kinds of people are those who think in pictures and visualize words in their minds. When you say words like dog, they do not see the letters d-o-g. Their minds show them an actual picture of a dog.

These people are keen on their appearance, which explains why they naturally stand up tall and dress smartly. They may have wrinkles in the forehead, which is usually indicative that they are scanning through your face and surrounding to see what they can visualize. Another thing they do is that they usually thin their lips and may also stiffen them, giving lots of eye contact.

Building rapport: To build a good rapport with them, you will have to give them a lot of eye contact and use words with many visual components like "I see what you mean;" "Picture this scenario…"

2. **The Listener**. These kinds of people are natural thinkers, and their brain thinks in words and sounds. They can be very creative and appreciate musical geniuses. When you are talking to them, they will usually look down to the left because you look when you are trying to process something. They are not too keen on dressing and appearance, and they will always not maintain eye-contact, or when they do, they may look lost while starring at you. Another thing they do is that they are likely to maintain telephone postures and mumble words to themselves. When they have a pen, they always click it or make

melody to every sound (or conversation) like internal drum beats.

Building Rapport: In other to do this, you don't give them too much eye contact as they may be uncomfortable, and when they are talking to you, they talk small and then look away. They may sometimes avoid confrontation and only speak back when they know you are genuinely listening to them. They will disconnect from you if they perceive you are not in the conversation.

In talking to them, you have to use auditory words, for example: "that sounds good…," "let's talk it over…" "I hear what you're saying…"

3. **The Toucher**. These kinds of people have a brain the thinks and processes things based on feelings and tactically. They are always ready to hug people and throw themselves in people's embrace (and embrace others too). They usually dress up for comfort rather than style, and their demeanor is always welcoming. They may be quick to always talk about how they feel, but then they are very forgiving. When having conversations, they tend to lean in because they want to close space, touch your arm so that they can be in close proximity. They look down a lot because that is where you look when you want to remember something you have felt before, as they usually process things based on feelings.

Building Rapport: Let them touch you if you feel comfortable, and if not, you give them a point of contact because an outright rejection may be damaging for them. When talking to them, you will need to use words that arouse their feelings like "Reach out and tell me..." "I want to hear what you feel about..."

Practice! Practice! Practice!

It is not enough to look through this book's pages, absorb all the information therein, and not do anything with that information. We must put them to practice if we are ever going to make a difference as a police officer. The key way to do that is to practice scenario-based exercises on each personality type based on previously discussed body language dynamics.

For example, how would you respond if you arrive at a scene, you are trying to have a conversation with a possible suspect, and they are trying to reach out to you and hold you?

What will be your response when you are trying to speak to a person as an officer of the law, and they seem to care less about what you are saying?

Armed with this knowledge of body language and non-verbal cues, how will you act differently from how you have been acting before?

Practice, they say, makes perfect. We do not get on a "hot scene" before we practice, we practice before we get to the place of action. This is because in the heat of the moment, what we have not practiced tends to be forgotten, but that which we have rehearsed over and over again, even in our heads, has a way of influencing our decisions or actions, even if the scenarios we are faced with are not the same.

Practice your craft, don't give in to the notion that you have been doing "This" for several years and don't need to make any worthwhile change to be better at what you do. The moment you stop growing, you start dying, and how do we grow, simply by practice. A person who puts in the hours practicing is far better than an expert who just believes in their expertise and refuses to learn something new every day.

A person could have all of the natural talents to become an exceptional police officer without practicing all they have learned during training. All that talent will never help them achieve mastery or be exceptional in their job as an officer. The truth is many outstanding police officers today do not often appear to have very much natural ability for the job on the surface. However, with constant practice, including personal and group practice, they have become outstanding at what they do.

Think about it, if we expect athletes, basketballers, footballers, etc. to perfect their crafts via practice, why should it be a strange idea to practice over and over again the lessons and training we may have gotten as police officers. The truth is, no excellent athlete depends solely on group practice to be able to excel at their craft; they put in hours and hours of personal practice to be outstanding in what they do.

Deliberate Practice

John Hayes is a cognitive psychology professor at Carnegie Mellon University. For several decades, he has been investigating the role of effort, practice, and knowledge in top performers in different fields. He studied people like Picasso and Mozart to determine precisely how long it took them to be exceptionally good at what they do and here is what he found out.

After analyzing several thousands of musical pieces produced around 1685 to 1900, Hayes developed a list of 500 pieces frequently played by symphonies worldwide and considered masterpieces. He discovered that 76 composers created the 500 popular pieces. He went ahead to map out each composer's career timeline and calculated how long they worked before creating their famous works.

He realized that, of the 500 popular pieces, only three were written in year eight and nine of their composer's career. The rest of the masterpieces were written after ten years of each of the composers professionally making music.

This study shows that without the composers putting in years of practice first, not a single piece of the time's outstanding music was created. Another striking thing that Hayes discovered is that their success was not merely a product of years of practice but that of years of deliberate practice.

In recent years, the practice habit of the late NBA star Kobe Bryant is one that provides a classic example of what deliberate practice is. In an article published by James Clear of jamesclear.com, he described what seems to be an encounter between Robert (a trainer for Team USA) and Kobe Bryant and reveals one reason he became successful at his craft.

Robert said,

> "I was invited to Las Vegas to help Team USA with their conditioning before they headed off

to London. I have had the opportunity to work with Carmelo Anthony and Dwayne Wade in the past, but this would be my first interaction with Kobe.

The night before the first scrimmage, I had just watched "Casablanca" for the first time, and it was about 3:30 AM.

A few minutes later, I was in bed, slowly fading away when I heard my cell ring. It was Kobe. I nervously picked up.

"Hey, uhh, Rob, I hope I'm not disturbing anything, right?"

"Uhh, no. What's up, Kob?"

"Just wondering if you could help me out with some conditioning work, that's all."

I checked my clock. 4:15 AM.

"Yeah, sure, I'll see you in the facility in a bit."

It took me about twenty minutes to get my gear and get out of the hotel. When I arrived and opened the room to the main practice floor, I saw Kobe. Alone. He was drenched in sweat as if he had just taken a swim. It was not even 5:00 AM.

We did some conditioning work for the next hour and fifteen minutes. Then, we entered the weight room, where he would do a multitude of strength training exercises for the next 45 minutes. After that, we parted ways. He went back to the practice floor to shoot. I went back to the hotel and crashed. Wow.

I had to be on the floor again at about 11:00 AM.

I woke up feeling sleepy, drowsy, and pretty much every side effect of sleep deprivation. (Thanks, Kobe.) I had a bagel and headed to the practice facility.

This next part, I remember very vividly. All of the Team USA players were there. LeBron was talking to Carmelo, and Coach Krzyzewski was trying to explain something to Kevin Durant. On the right side of the practice facility, Kobe was by himself shooting jumpers.

I went over to him, patted him on the back, and said, "Good work this morning."

"Huh?"

"Like, the conditioning. Good work."

"Oh. Yeah, thanks, Rob. I really appreciate it."

"So, when did you finish?"

"Finish what?"

"Getting your shots up. What time did you leave the facility?"

"Oh, just now. I wanted 800 makes. So yeah, just now."

For those of you keeping track at home, Kobe Bryant started his conditioning work around 4:30 am, continued to run and sprint until 6 am, lifted weights from 6 am to 7 am, and finally made 800 jump shots between 7 am and 11 am.

Oh yeah, and then Team USA had practice."

Malcolm Gladwell popularized the idea that 10,000 hours of practice makes one an expert in that field. Thus, making people believe that once they spend a year or two at a job or working as a police officer, they know all there is to know about police work.

The truth is there is more to practice than just putting in the 10,000 hours or spending a year or two at the job, so we are no longer referred to as a "Rookie." We need to be deliberate about practicing our craft irrespective of how long we have been in the police force because the way we practice is just as important as how much time we've practiced.

Anders Ericsson, in his book *Peak: Secrets from The New Science of Expertise*, said this of deliberate practice

"The hallmark of purposeful or deliberate practice is that you try to do something that you cannot do — that takes you out of your comfort zone- and that you practice it over and over

again, focusing on exactly how you are doing it, where you are falling short, and how you can get better."

He also made this assertion about deliberate and purposeful practice that I believe is very true when he wrote;

> *"Deliberate practice involves well-defined, specific goals and often involves improving some aspect of the target performance; it is not aimed at some vague overall improvement. Once an overall goal has been set, a teacher or coach will develop a plan for making a series of small changes that will add up to the desired larger change. Improving some aspect of the target performance allows a performer to see that his or her performances have been improved by the training. Deliberate practice is deliberate, that is, it requires a person's full attention and conscious actions. It isn't enough to simply follow a teacher's or coach's directions. The student must concentrate on the specific goal for his or her practice activity so that adjustments can be made to control practice."*

As the name suggests, deliberate practice is intentional, focused, and requires that you push outside your comfort zone until you're better at the work you do. As cops, we should not just wake up every day and go for the rest of our work life. We must deliberately practice, practice, and practice our craft until we get better at it.

Chapter 7

Understand and Respond

When it comes to interacting with a suspect in a crime scene or having a conversation with a victim, one of the key aspects of communication, we must learn to implement listening to understand before responding. As law enforcement officers, we sometimes swing into action because of the urgency of the situation that we sometimes fail to effectively listen to understand before we respond to a query, questions, or words of a person or suspect is saying to us.

When we fail to clearly understand the information a person is trying to pass across before swinging into action based on what we "perceive" the situation to be, we often make a wrong judgment in that situation or even escalate it further into a hostile situation. The truth is we cannot afford to make mistakes in our judgment when we find ourselves at a crime scene or when someone is brought in for processing because such mistakes could mean the life of that person. It, therefore, becomes easier for us to at least listen first to understand; more like process the information that we have received before acting or responding to the situation

Our actions and the response we give to an issue are often dependent on our understanding of the prevailing circumstances even before we arrive at the scene. When we understand what had gone on before we arrived at a scene, we stand a better chance of responding appropriately and in such a way that will not be harmful or detrimental to the life of those around us.

For example, when trying to engage a suspect who we are confident does not have any firearm or poses no harm or danger to us. Even if convinced, they are in the right. We must take the time to engage them in a dialogue in such a way that shows them that we understand or at least are trying to understand their point of view even though we may still need to put them under arrest.

One of the greatest needs of every human, including suspects, is to be understood. Everyone wants to be respected and valued irrespective of who they are, their skin color, or our perception of their personality. However, it is unfortunate that one of our innate tendencies as police officers is to want to solve people's problems as quickly as possible, sometimes to the detriment of fully understanding what the problem is. When we take the time to understand someone instead of judging them based on our views or bias of their personality, they are more inclined to drop their defenses and be open to influence.

To understand someone and respond effectively and accordingly, we must first learn to genuinely listen to them to understand their view before responding and not just waiting for our turn to talk. When people talk, we often hear them but are not listening to them because we are usually too busy in our heads preparing a response, judging them and their actions, or filtering their words through our own paradigms.

Even though we have talked about the importance of listening in a previous chapter and have even shown us how to listen to others properly, we look at how not listening correctly could be a barrier to understanding a person and de-escalating a hostile situation.

Barriers to Understanding before responding.

Over time, I have realized that when we misunderstand people as a police officer, we often engaged or used the following poor listening skills, which are barriers to understanding them when speaking with them. These barriers to understanding include: Zoning Out, Pretend Listening, Selective Listening, Word Listening, and Self-centered Listening.

- **Zoning Out** – When a person is talking to us, and we ignore them, or we fail to acknowledge what they are saying, we have zoned out on them, and our mind is on something else. For example, when on a traffic stop, we see a person put their hand in the glove compartment while talking to us, we often zone out on the words they are saying and are more concerned about what their hands are doing. In some quarters, one of the reasons the George Floyd incident happened was because the Police officer who had his knee on his neck zoned out on him while he was on the floor. If he had just been consciously present and listening to what the man had to say, we probably would not have had the ripple effect of that incident.

Zoning out on a person while they are speaking means you have no interest in what they are saying. It shows that you care less about reaching a fair and understandable conclusion before responding. You are probably just there to do your job and not try to understand if there is an alternative stance to the bias preconceived notion over the radio or by an informant.

We have all seen videos or witnessed where a person has been arrested on the charges of car theft, misdemeanor, property damage, or charges like that only to discover it was a case of mistaken identity. The individual often gets arrested not because they did not make any attempt to prove that they are innocent but most times because the police officers zone out on them and the information they're trying to pass across, only to be

For example, recently, a man is suing a South Georgian city and its police department for excessive use of force after being body-slammed in a case of mistaken identity. Someone had called in a case of suspicious activity within their neighborhood; the police arrived at the scene, saw the man, and instantly assumed he was the one causing the disturbance. While one of the officers was busy questioning him about what he was doing in that environment, another officer who had no clue of what had been transpiring between the first cop and the man, came slowly from behind and, without listening to the conversation, body-slammed him on the ground; all captured on camera.

Later the sergeant who slammed the man to the ground said he thought the 47 years old was a suspect in a panhandling case. The sergeant in question said the suspected man was "Standing in a bladed stance" and had appeared to be arguing or debating with the patrol officer, so he assumed he was the suspect. According to his Federal Lawsuit against the South Georgian City and its police department, the man suffered distal radial and ulnar fractures in the incident, and his civil rights violated. The second officer could have avoided the entire incident had he taken the time to listen to understand and not just react or respond

- **Hearing**: With listening comes understanding; however, some police officers pretend to listen when all they are doing is hearing from you. They are present with you but are not paying much attention to what you are saying. They say different phrases like "Yeah," "Oh," "Mm-hmm," because they understand the "Tricks" of communication and want to appear to be listening to you when in reality, they are not. It is one thing to hear a person speak and a very different ball game when listening to them. For example, a man could pretend to be listening to his wife while he listens to the evening news. He could be responding to her in a monosyllabic manner while, in reality, he honestly does want to end the conversation and move on to pay full attention to the evening news. So while he may be hearing her speak, he truly isn't listening to her; he had his attention divided all along.

It is also with us as cops; sometimes, we tend to hear a person speak but not listen to them. For example, when a person calls the police to what is seemingly a misunderstanding between them and their partner, some police officers tend to hear the other party – especially if they are a man- but not really listen to them. This partiality happens because we – and even society in general – sometimes have the bias that when there is a domestic case between a man and a woman, the man is usually at fault.

Hearing, simply put, is the act of perceiving a sound by ear and respond to it by reflex while listening is something you consciously choose to do. Listening requires attention and concentration so that your brain processes meanings from words and sentences. Hearing a person has more to do with the physiological act of perceiving sound from them than it is about making sense and connecting with the person speaking on a deeper level.

Even though hearing may be the first step to listening and understanding, the two are very different. Hearing is like collecting data while listening goes further to process that data before returning with a response or output that will improve mutual understanding and foster cooperation.

A straightforward way to know whether you are listening or just hearing a person is to look at your response to the person speaking. A quick give away is when your response is monosyllabic.

When you have genuinely listened to what a person has to say, your response to them will often be detailed and somewhat of a rephrase of the information given to you in such a way that shows you have processed the information received.

For example, in the case of the man who was pretending to be listening to his wife while watching the evening news. His response to her will go beyond yes, no, oh, really to something like, "Do you mean you had to wait in line before being attended to at the checkout point?" or "How did you eventually move the groceries from the store to the car?" He will never be able to respond in bits because he truly listened and has processed the information.

Do you want to see another classic example of hearing in action? Look at your local politicians, especially those who find it difficult to say much to their audience via town hall meetings or gatherings like that but know how to nod, smile, and grunt in all the right places. They have perfected the art of hearing but are not taking anything in. Their goal with their constituents is to make a good impression, especially during an election year, and then move on, probably never to talk to them again once the elections are over.

- **Partial Listening** – Agreed, it is not every information we encounter that is of interest to us. So, when we are talking to a person, and they say things that do not interest us, we tend to zone out briefly and then return attention to them when they say something that catches our interest.

For example, we have all being in a situation where someone is saying something to us, and all we were doing is "Hearing" them but not listening to them. Suddenly they say something that triggers our attention, and we say, "Come again?" or "Pardon, what was the last thing you said?"

Partial listening is ubiquitous today because of the short attention span of this generation. People no longer have the patience to give attention to something that does not interest them even though it might be necessary. According to research carried out by Microsoft, the average human being now has an attention span of eight seconds. A sharp decrease from the average attention span of twelve seconds in the year 2000; if accurate, a goldfish's attention span is longer than that of humans today.

A study published in 2019 by some researchers at the Technical University of Denmark suggests that humans' global attention span is narrowing down due to the sheer amount of information available to binge. According to Sune Lehmann, a professor from the Technical University of Denmark who worked on the study, "It seems that the allocated attention time in our collective minds has a certain size, but the cultural items competing for that attention have become more densely packed."

In partial listening, police officers often listen to the other person with the best intentions and become distracted either by stray thoughts or by something someone else is doing around the scene. The problem with this type of listening is that when the officer was distracted, it could be essential or pivotal to how they respond to the situation; thus, when they miss out on it, their judgment of the situation becomes grossly skewed.

When you were talking to someone, and they only paid attention to the part that interested them.

- **Word Picking**- When we talk with someone and are only concerned about the things they say and not the emotional structure of what is said, we are merely listening to your words. As has been established, the words people speak is not all there is to communication. There is the non-verbal part that must be intentionally put into consideration when we are speaking to people.

THE HARDEST LANGUAGE

When listening to people, we have to go beyond just hearing words with our ears to listen with our eyes and heart, since only a small percentage of said words communicate the situation. The tone and body language of the person behind those words count for much. Therefore, to hear what other people are really saying, we need to listen to what they are not saying.

When we word listen to people without considering the tone and body language, we often misread or misinterpret what a person is saying. Consider these two statements;

"I stole..."

&

"I stole?"

Both are the same words but mean very different things. One is a confirmation of action, while the other is a rhetorical question.

Therefore, to become a genuine listener as a police officer, we sometimes need to take off our shoes and stand in others.' Communication is not a competition of words where each one is looking to say the most or have the last words.

Ideally, both parties can be correct when people communicate because they see the issue from their different perspectives. The ability to balance what is said, the emotions and body language behind the words, and what the law says should make us unique as cops.

Selective Listening - This involves listening for particular things and ignoring others. We thus hear what we want to hear and pay little attention to 'extraneous' detail. Here we listen from our biased perspective, hoping to hear them say things that confirm our suspicions without giving attention to the other things mentioned.

A person who does this type of listening will not evaluate or process some of the information passed across to them but will choose to stick with whatever part of that information confirms their thoughts and then act on it. When we engage in this type of listening, we often jump to conclusions without listening to everything the speaker says.

For example, acting on a tip-off, a police officer confronted a man driving a black Mercedes Benz to know if the car belonged to him. The moment he said No and without listening to the next things he had to say, the police officer pulled out his gun and placed him under arrest only to realize later that the car belonged to the man's friend and he had given it to him to help him get gas.

As police officers, jumping to a conclusion without being patient to get the whole picture can be very harmful. It can create a barrier in the communication process because sometimes the speaker is not planning to make a point that you think they will make.

THE HARDEST LANGUAGE

Effective communication between a police officer and a suspect plays a critical role in de-escalating any intense situation. It also, to a large, determines how a suspect responds or acts toward us. When people sense that the person, they are communicating with is making an effort to understand them, they are willing to open up even the more to them and be more relaxed in the way they react.

People often spend much time reading, writing, or even taking down statements but do not give much attention to listening, which undoubtedly is an essential skill in police work even much more than speaking.

Chapter 8

What would you do?

One of the primary purposes of law enforcement agencies is to uphold the laws of the land. Our duties as officers of these law enforcement agencies are to see that our jurisdiction laws are upheld at all times and irrespective of who is involved.

But what happens when we find ourselves in a situation where the laws of the land are seemingly in contradiction to our personal beliefs, or we find ourselves in a dilemma where we are caught between acting right according to the law or acting fair as a human? What would we do when faced with two seemingly serious and urgent situations that require our attention and action? What would we do when we are confronted with a hostile situation but are ill-equipped at the moment to confront it? Thus, as outlined in this chapter, the need for scenario-based questions helps us prepare for such a time as this even before we encounter them.

The essence of these scenario-based types of questions is to help us think through, in a relaxed environment, how we will respond to certain real-life situations like law enforcement officers based on the information at our disposal and not necessarily to see who is right wrong.

Therefore, when we try to answer these questions, we must be as detailed as possible as a yes or no answer will not help us see the reason or motive behind our answers. So, take the time to think through the questions, write down what your response or action will be in such a situation, and then explain the rationale behind that action or decision.

In going through the questions, you will face situations that seem like two or more possible ways to handle it. In that case, feel free to write down the most applicable line of action you will take considering the situation and then explain your reason for choosing to go that route.

In my opinion, I will suggest that you do not just blurt out or write down the first thought that comes to mind. Consider if there are alternative actions that you can take. The truth, this is your opportunity to practice your actions or reaction before you hit the field; after all, it is not a test of how fast you can respond to the situation but how well you do. So, take your time and give some thought to what you are about to say or write down. The truth is, the rationale behind your action is as important as the action itself, so try as much as you can to incorporate that in your answer.

Carmelo Rodriguez

I expect that the questions in this chapter will be fun to answer, so enjoy it while working at it. You can read this in a group together with your fellow officers and then work out your answers together. Group exercises are very beneficial as they could help check your answers to verify how relevant to the situation it is.

In a group setting, answers may vary from person to person, not because they are wrong but because they look into the situation from a different point of view from yours. So, feel free to let everyone answer the questions as truthfully and to the best of your knowledge as possible and then review each other's answers to find out what their views or biases are related to that situation.

The goal of scenario-based questions is to help you tackle problems from real-life situations that police officers may encounter, so it's unnecessary to have encountered the situation first hand before you can answer correctly. It is a test to help you figure out what your best line of action will be should you find yourself in such a situation, so go ahead and answer all questions.

The questions in this chapter cover a wide range of scenarios, such as the use of force, integrity, supervision, judgment, and interaction with co-workers in the line of duty. They are in a randomized order; you can figure out in which area what question is trying to test and then answer appropriately. There are 35 questions in all, covering each area of consideration listed above.

Some questions are taken from real-life police interview training portals known to help potential police officers prepare

THE HARDEST LANGUAGE

for their police interviews, so they are real-life situations that other officers have faced in times past.

Below are the questions:

1) You arrive at a report of a burglary at a convenience store. The store is closed for the night. After you and your backup officer check out the store, it appears that the person has stolen the register drawer and is nowhere around. Dispatch tells you that the store owner is on his way to assess the damage. While waiting, your fellow officer opens a package of chips and eats them and throws the bag away. He then takes a few candy bars off the shelf and puts them in his patrol car. He says that the owner will never miss them. What do you do?

2) During a traffic stop, the driver of the car seems inebriated and smells of alcohol. When you initiate a field sobriety test, the driver fails. As you are preparing to take the offender to jail, he tells you that he is the city manager's son. He tells you that he will make sure that his father has you fired if you take him to jail. What do you do?

3) You have conducted a traffic stop, and you're in the middle of issuing a traffic citation when a violent crime in progress in your assigned area comes over the radio. What course of action would you take?

4) You and your partner arrest a subject for a theft at a local department store. After the subject is handcuffed and taken into custody and placed in the back of your patrol car, as you are getting ready to leave, the suspect begins calling your partner names. Your partner opens the door and punches the suspect in the face and walks away. What do you do?

5) You are assigned to conduct traffic enforcement in a local school zone because of numerous complaints of speeders in the area. You observe a car traveling at a high rate of speed and effect a traffic stop. When you get up to the driver's window, you find that the driver is your mother-in-law. What course of action would you take?

6) You are on patrol in a business district at 2:00 am when you find the front door of a business that appeared to be pried open. What do you do first?

7) You and a fellow officer are eating lunch at a local restaurant. After finishing the meal, the waitress brings you the bill, and you find that she did not charge you, and the waitress tells you that your meal is free. What would you do?

8) You and another officer respond to a burglary call at a home. As you go through the house and find no one there, you observe your partner take a $20 bill off a dresser and put it in his pocket. No one else witnesses this but you. How would you address this situation?

9) One of the officers on your squad, who is a very good friend of yours, shows up for work and you smell beer on his breath. You believe that he has been drinking. You also believe that this officer, who is your friend, has a drinking problem. What are you going to do?

10) In this state, it is mandatory that you make an arrest when a domestic battery occurs. You respond to a domestic violence call, and upon arrival, you discover that the male in the situation is a police officer with another local law enforcement agency. The female is claiming he beat her and has several

marks on her face consistent with being beaten. Your investigation is consistent with her story. He takes you aside and tells you that he cannot go to jail, or he will lose his career as a police officer. After you finish speaking with him, he approaches you again and says that she does not want to press charges and begs you not to arrest him. Explain what you would do?

11) You are dispatched to a fight in progress at a local bar. When you arrive, you see that the fight is still in progress. What actions would you take to stop the fight?

12) You are off duty at a party when you notice several of the partygoers begin to smoke marijuana. What would you do?

13) You are patrolling your assigned area when you see what appears to be a shop owner in front of his store with a gun in his hand.

14) You get called to a home because someone believed child abuse was going on. You hear a child crying in the home, but the man will not allow you and tells you to get a warrant when you ask to come in. What do you do?

15) You are dispatched to a traffic accident. Put these three things in the order you would do them and give a reason for doing so: control traffic, check for injuries, interview witnesses.

16) You respond to back up another unit in an alley. When you arrive, you see a man running away, and the officer at the scene is yelling at you, "Shoot him, shoot him," what will you do?

17) You are flagged down by a woman in a parking lot. The woman tells you that she found her son playing with a gun and she would like you to have a talk with her son about the dangers of playing with guns. What do you do?

18) You and your partner are driving a dangerous prisoner to the jail. While en route to the jail, you observe an accident involving three vehicles. It appears that damage to the vehicles is significant. What would you do?

19) While off duty, you go to a convenience store to purchase a few items. No one in the store knows you are a police officer. While you are paying for the items, the cashier engages in a conversation with you. She mentions that the believes she received a counterfeit twenty-dollar bill today. What would you do?

20) For the past several months, there have been many assignments that required someone to work late at night. Everyone in your office has done their share of working late hours except for one person. His continual refusal to work after hours is causing a strain with his co-workers. What would you do?

21) You and your partners are executing a search warrant on a suspected drug dealer's residence. Your team finds illegal drugs and a large amount of money in the house. As your team is securing the contraband in the appropriate evidence bags, you observe one team member place some of the money into his pocket. What would you do?

22) You are investigating the illegal copying and selling of videotaped movies. While interviewing the owner of one of

the suspected video stores, he offers you several free rentals. What would you do?

23) Everyone in your office has had the chance to participate in a special assignment. When another detail comes up, your supervisor gives it to a co-worker who has already been on a similar assignment. This pattern continues two more times with you getting passed over for any special assignment. What would you do?

24) After working in one office for five years, you receive a new supervisor. After six months under her supervision, it appears that she does not like you. You discuss this with her, but she acts like nothing will change. At the end of the year, she gives you a low rating. You talk to her about your rating, but she appears to be inattentive. What would you do?

25) You are by yourself driving through an area that has several retail stores. You witness a man grab a woman's purse. The two of them are struggling for control of the purse. The man starts to strike the woman with his hands. What would you do?

26) You and several other officers are attempting to arrest a subject at his residence. As you are walking up to the house, the front door opens, and the subject appears. He steps out of the doorway and onto the front porch. He has a gun in his hand, and he begins shooting at you. What would you do?

27) Two co-workers in your office do not like each other. Their refusal to work together is causing problems in scheduling assignments. Morale in the office is low because of their bickering. What would you do?

28) You are in a high-speed chase when you come upon railroad tracks. The railroad lights are flashing, and the crossing bars are moving down with a train at full speed closing in and you see the suspect barrel through the crossing bars. Do you proceed in the chase?

29) You are off duty at a friend's party. While at this party, you observe several individuals who you do not recognize using illegal substances. What do you do?

30) You respond to a call about an alleged suicide attempt. You walk into a room where you see a person seated holding a gun to their head. The person states that if you leave, he/she will shoot themselves, but if you stay, he/she will shoot you. What do you do?

31) You and a fellow officer responded to a domestic incident, and when preparing to leave the scene, you notice your partner taking a small item of value from the home and putting it in his pocket. What do you do?

32) You respond to a call to assist another officer and arrive as the officer is placing the cuffed suspect into his patrol car. After placing the suspect in the car, you witness the officer punch the suspect. What do you do?

33) You are called to the scene of a loud party at a private residence and after arriving, notice the underage son of your best friend in the corner of the room holding an alcoholic beverage. What do you do?

34) Due to excessive work on a given assignment, someone needs to work late hours. Everybody in the office has done

their share of late shifts except for one person who is refusing to do so. The burden becomes unevenly distributed among you and your colleagues, and you see that there is tension. What would you do?

35) You are investigating a store for possibly selling fake items such as bags, shoes, clothes copying a famous brand. The owner offers to give you a discount voucher to use for yourself or your family for any future purchases in the store. What would you do?

Answering all 35 questions in this chapter helps us determine ahead of time what your reaction will be in specific scenarios and helps you reframe them if you realize they are not exactly in line with the guidelines of law enforcement. For example, the judgment scenario questions focus on helping you determine if your decisions or actions are or will be right when carrying out your duties. In contrast, the use of force scenario questions focuses on determining if you understand how much force, i.e., using a gun and other weapons you have at your disposal - you are allowed to apply while doing your job.

The supervision scenario questions in this chapter help determine your reactions in dealing with a conflict between you and your supervisor, and if you can adequately relate or deal with a superior in a misunderstanding situation.

The integrity scenario questions help determine your level of honesty and how much a moral person you are as a police officer.

It checks to see if you are a straight-up truthful person or can bend the rules depending on the crime's individual. Interaction with co-worker's scenario questions helps determine how your presence in a team affects the group dynamics and how you will act in a conflict between you and a co-worker.

Therefore, it is important that you take the time to review the questions and answer them because that will bring to your consciousness your actions and help you determine what your new line of action will be should you find yourself wanting in some areas.

Chapter 9

Where Your Power Lies

In the previous chapter, we recreated so many scenarios that officers get to face from time to time. I hope you took the time to answer those questions, giving thought to your natural predisposition and how you are supposed to act in such a situation based on the new knowledge you have at your disposal. But, irrespective of how you responded to the questions, there's something I hope you took notice of, and that is where your power as a police officer truly lies.

As an officer of the law, we frequently mistake our true power for the weapons we are armed with, and yes, those weapons can come in handy when in a hostile or hot situation. However, much more than the batons and the guns we carry, there is a more significant weapon that we have at our disposal, which, when used correctly, can disarm even the biggest of all threats, especially in non-lethal situations.

The truth is, we have been made to erroneously belief — sometimes even by the community we have vowed to protect — that without the guns and Tasers we carry about, we cannot effectively carry out our functions as cops. We have a false belief that we can only command the community's respect when we act with our weapons.

For example, we have all seen or at least heard of people who try to disrespect or attack a police officer because they think he is unarmed, making that officer erroneously believe that the respect they command within the community is because they carry a gun around.

We need not give in to that false belief because here is one fact that I know and have experienced personally, we as officers do not need to carry a physical weapon to be powerful before a group of people. Our strength is not in those material things we carry about as weapons but in our mouth. The way we use that mouth can make a difference in the way people within a community perceive and act toward us.

For example, picture these two scenarios and tell me what you think brought about the change or escalated the situation into a more deadly one than it should have been.

Scenario 1

You are called into a scene where someone who has a mental health issue is having an out of control episode and is going off threatening those in his immediate environment. You get to the scene, and you see other officers pointing their guns at him, yelling, and threatening to shoot him if he does not drop his weapon.

Rather than yelling out at him or using brute force as the other officers are threatening to do, you see another officer who, like you, just arrived at the scene. He signaled his colleagues to lower their weapons, went a little bit closer, and communicated effectively with the enraged man. He spoke in a lower tone and tried using a calm demeanor to speak with the man; to find out what was happening, how he can help, and change his mind and drop the weapon he has with him.

From his conversation with the enraged man, he discovers he was simply having a bad day and was overwhelmed with a lot of emotions coupled with his mental health issues. He speaks further with him and shows him he understands what he is going through by putting himself in his shoes and speaking words that show empathy toward his situation. He feels a lot better, all the while crying because he feels a sense of remorse for what he has done, drops his weapon, goes down on his knees with his hands visibly shown to the officer, and was willingly ready for arrest.

Scenario 2

You are just a regular citizen in a scene of an ongoing candlelight vigil held outside a police headquarters. Every concerned and angry citizen has gathered demanding answers, information, and justice regarding the shootings that occurred just a few days ago, leaving another man dead. That man, for this book, will be referred to as John Doe.

Earlier in the day, the police chief, who spoke to the press, gave a "No comment" answer to almost all the pertinent questions asked regarding the shooting and refused to provide any details whatsoever as to what happened during the shooting of John Doe.

Right there on the candlelight scene, you had the opportunity to speak to a few of the protesters who have identified themselves as family and friends of the deceased John Doe. One of them, who identified himself as the brother to this deceased John Doe, says to you he believes that the police officers used a taser on John before eventually shooting him to death. Another family member says to you that even though John was a troubled man and was going through some difficult times in his life, there was no reason for the police to shoot him; thus, he perceives a cover-up somewhere.

Right before your eyes, a peaceful protest that started as a demand for answers to the shooting of John Doe over the next few days evolves into large-scale disturbances which further resulted in major clashes between the large group of protesters and the police, with rocks and bottles thrown at the police and the police officers using teargas and pepper spray to disperse the crowd.

Damage to several downtown area businesses, many people – including the police officers – have been injured, and several overnight arrests. Despite the seemingly hostile situation, the police continued to work to establish order in the downtown area so that while things seem relatively calm in the morning, tensions remain very high.

THE HARDEST LANGUAGE

While you may not be able to say precisely what happened at the shooting scene, in your own opinion, what or who do you think escalated the situation and with what weapon?

In fact, in both scenarios, who do you think will be more respected or appreciated for their actions? The first officer for sure. What do you think was responsible for the de-escalation of one situation and the escalation of the other? On the other hand, what do you think was responsible for the enraged man dropping his weapon? In the second scenario, the situation spiraled into riots and destruction of property? Simply put, the words spoken.

In one situation, the officer involved was fully aware of where his true power lies, while the other does not understand that his mouth is a powerful weapon. Therein lies his power; thus, misused situations can cause manageable situations to degenerate into out of control situations.

The truth is we can almost always handle any non-life-threatening situation by what we and how we say it.

Our language and style of communication are as important as what we say. People want to hear us speak to them with respect and not with a mental assumption that we are higher than they are; thus, they deserve no explanation.

A worthy example

We are police officers who have been called to serve people, which means that those people have the right to hear us speak to them and answer their questions in the most humane way possible. It is the right of every individual to know the reason for their arrest. Still, when a police officer goes ahead to arrest a person without telling them why, that can result in a struggle that can further degenerate into a hostile situation.

For example, In New South Wales in Australia, apart from a few exceptions, the police must make a lawful announcement of an arrest before going ahead to do so. Failure to make the announcement will mean that the officer is not acting in the execution of their duty. Not acting in the execution of duty represents a good substantive defense to resist arrest and assault police charges.

According to the Law Enforcement (Powers and Responsibilities) Act of 2002 (NSW), any police officer making an arrest must:

(a) Provide evidence that they are a police officer (unless they are in uniform)

(b) The name of the police officer and his / her place of duty

(c) The reason for the exercise of the power of arrest

The requirements (a) and (b) above go further than the common law. Thus, a police officer who does not comply with all of the above is not acting to execute his / her duty.

The few exceptions to the statute above are where it is not practical for the police officer to immediately provide evidence that they are indeed an officer of the law they could go ahead and arrest. However, they must provide that evidence as soon as it is reasonably practical to do so. In addition, where two or more police officers are arresting, only one must provide the evidence while the other officers must give their name and place of duty if asked.

Mark Dennis of Forbes Chambers in his document "The measure of Last Resort" (June 2011 edition) says that this common law has as its foundational case Christie vs. Leachinsky [1947] AC 573, 1 All ER 567, and in particular the judgment of Viscount Simon at 587---588:

(1) If a police officer arrests without a warrant upon reasonable suspicion of a felony or other crime of a sort that does not require a warrant, he must inform the person arrested of the true ground of arrest in ordinary circumstances. He is not entitled to keep the reason to himself or give a reason that is not the actual reason. A seized citizen is entitled to the knowledge of what charge or suspicion of what crime he allegedly committed.

(2) If the citizen is not so informed but is nevertheless seized, the policeman, apart from certain exceptions, is liable for false imprisonment.

(3) The requirement that the person arrested should be informed of the reason why he is seized naturally does not exist if the circumstances are such that he must know the general nature of the alleged offense for which he is detained.

(4) The requirement that he should be so informed does not mean that technical or precise language need be used. The matter is a matter of substance, and turns on the elementary proposition that in this country a person is, prima facie, entitled to his freedom and is only required to submit to

restraints on his freedom if he knows in substance the reason why it is claimed that this restraint should be imposed.

(5) The person arrested cannot complain that he has not been supplied with the above information as and when he should be, if he himself produces the situation which makes it practically impossible to inform him, e.g., by immediate counter---attack or by running away. There may well be other exceptions to the general rule in addition to those I have indicated, and the above propositions are not intended to constitute a formal or complete code but to indicate the general principles of our law on a very important matter. These principles equally apply to a private person who arrests on suspicion. If a policeman who entertained a reasonable suspicion that X has committed a felony were at liberty to arrest him and march him off to a police station without giving any explanation of why he was doing this, the prima facie right of personal liberty would be gravely infringed."

Another worthy passage can be found in the judgment of Lord Simonds at 591:

> "Is citizen A bound to submit unresistingly to arrest by citizen B in ignorance of the charge made against him? I think, my Lords, that cannot be the law of England. Blind, unquestioning obedience is the law of tyrants and slaves: it does not yet flourish on English soil."

Look at these fine laws stating categorically where an officer's power lies; however, has that stopped the violent encounters between citizens and police in New South Wales? I don't think so. And why is that? In my opinion, that is because police officers are yet to realize where their power truly lies, their words entirely.

Think about it, if you're expected by law to announce before carrying out an arrest, where then do you think your power truly lies?

In the US, based on the ruling of the U.S. Supreme between Miranda v. Arizona, after making an arrest, the police must inform a detainee of their fifth amendment and Sixth amendment rights for statements made during questioning be admissible. Failure to do so means that nothing they say in those following moments will be admissible when brought before a judge in the law court.

The truth is, it should not matter what our natural disposition to a group of people may be as individuals. As soon as we put on the uniform or carry on the badge as police officers, we must understand that we are not just representing ourselves. Still, the law and government and the government owe its citizen an explanation for their actions.

When police officers refuse to talk, it opens the door for speculations and false assumptions that can make people see us in a bad light. These speculations and assumptions are based on emotions and innuendos and not on facts more often than not.

Our power is in our mouth and not our hip.

Chapter 10

The Last Resort

On New Year's Eve of 2016, officers from a municipal police department got a call to investigate the report of a disturbed man armed with a gun in an apartment. The person who took the call did an outstanding job collecting as much information as possible and continued to send back essential details to the responding officers. They immediately established a perimeter and called for a crisis intervention trained officer even before trying to make contact with the armed man.

More intelligence on the state of mind and access to a weapon by the suspect were gathered from his family members by officers on the scene, and an ambulance tactically kept nearby. After assessing things, the officers, concerned about other residents, began clearing the vicinity and moving them to a safe zone. The suspect, who was initially shielded by a part of the apartment's balcony, began shooting at the officers. He shot and killed one officer before being shot and killed himself.

XXXXX

On a spring evening in 2018, an officer who was on duty initiated a traffic stop on a vehicle for an unknown traffic violation. The vehicle occupants were a female driver and a male passenger seated on the passenger's seat in front. The officer approached the vehicle and requested the driver's license and the passenger's identifying information.

Both provided the requested information, and the officer quickly ran a criminal warrant check on both individuals. The query into the driver's status returned with no warrants, but the passenger's information returned as false or inaccurate. To clarify the male passenger's information, the officer made a passenger-side approach to interview the male. It is unknown what was said, but a physical altercation between the suspect and the officer occurred. During this altercation, the suspect produced a semiautomatic handgun and shot the officer multiple times. During this incident, the female driver was shot in the foot and was left at the scene by the suspect.

Overhearing the gunfire, civilians in the area responded to the scene to render aid to the officer. One citizen used the officer's shoulder microphone to radio for assistance. After transportation to the hospital, the officer died a short time later.

The officer was not aware that the suspect, later apprehended the next day, was wanted for a string of armed robberies and parole violations.

XXXXX

For scenarios like this and others like it, the use of force has become the last resort for us as police officers. The truth is, while we may continue to advocate for the use of voice over force, we can never totally rule out the need for the use of force in some situations like the ones described above and as shown in the report below.

According to a study of Law Enforcement Fatalities Between 2010-2016 carried out by Nick Breul and Desiree Luongo that released in December 2017, the following are a part of the summary of its findings:

Calls for Service

1) Calls related to *Domestic Disputes* and domestic-related incidents represented the highest number of fatal types of calls for service. They were also the underlying cause of several other service calls that resulted in law enforcement fatalities, including some ambushes.

2) 17 of the 18 examined cases involving a *Domestic Disputes* call involved officers fired upon outside the residence or dispatched location. Six of those cases involved officers being engaged by gunfire from over 50 feet.

3) A Man with a Gun and *Shots Fired* call types both increased dramatically over the numbers found in the first analysis of Fatal Calls and Deadly Encounters. Those two firearm-related calls for service nearly doubled and in a shorter period than that covered in the initial report.

4) In 43 percent of all the cases in which officers were responding to a dispatched call for service that ended in a fatality, the officers had been advised the suspect(s) might be armed, or they had made prior threats. This number represents calls from all the categories.

5) 30 percent, officers were alone when they were shot and killed, answering a call for service.

In the Self-Initiated Enforcement Activity segment of the report, it stated that

1) Fifty-two percent of officers killed while engaged in Self-Initiated Activity conducted a traffic stop for vehicle enforcement. It remained the most common enforcement action that results in an officer's fatality.

2) In 49 percent of the cases involving an officer initiating a stop on a vehicle, they were shot and killed as the driver and passengers' interaction began. In 21 percent, the officer was shot and killed before contacting the driver.

3) Officers are at a disadvantage as they contact suspicious persons and drivers because they cannot predict how the suspect(s) will react or fully understand the situation to which they are responding.

4) Of all the cases studied involving slain officers, suspects used handguns in 71 percent of the cases, a rifle in 21 percent, and shotguns in 8 percent.

Ambushes

1) The year 2016 saw a significant increase in ambush attacks on unsuspecting officers, as 21 were shot and killed. In two significant cases, Dallas, and Baton Rouge, suspects intentionally targeting law enforcement killed multiple officers.

2) Eighty-one officers were shot and killed in ambushes over the seven-year period from 2010-2016 that was studied.

3) Sixty-one percent of the officers shot and killed by means of an ambush attack were not answering a call for service or engaged in enforcement action or performing official duties. Twelve of the officers were assassinated as they sat in their patrol cars.

4) Nearly half of the fatal assaults were carried out by suspects armed with rifles.

5) *Domestic Dispute* calls were the predominant calls for service that resulted in an ambush shooting of responding officers.

6) Fourteen officers were shot and killed while off-duty. Angry defendants or targets of criminal investigations attacked those officers on their way home or even at their homes.

The Ideal Society

Do people often clamor for an ideal society where law enforcement does not have to use force to compel people to act accordingly? Is that practicable seeing the rate at which police officers get killed? While I understand their sentiments about a force-free intervention by the police, the question is, will every citizen out there be willing to comply with the police? The answer to that question is no because there will always be those who will not comply with society's law and will do anything within their powers for them not to be taken into custody, even if it means killing the officers involved.

For example, on a February morning in the western part of the country, with the snow-covered ground, the county sheriff's office received a report of a man walking along a busy street with what appeared to be a handgun. After the dispatcher broadcast the report and description of the suspect and travel direction, deputies set off. A short time later, a deputy notified the dispatcher that he had contacted an individual matching the description provided.

The deputy encountered the young suspect as he crossed the street and stopped him to question him. The suspect asked if he was being detained, and when the deputy informed him that he was, the teenage suspect attempted to flee, and the deputy deployed his Taser, causing the suspect to fall to the ground. Once the Electronic Control Device had completed delivering its energy, the deputy moved to handcuff the suspect. The suspect resisted and pulled a pistol from his waistband, shot the deputy standing over him, and struck him three times.

The teenage suspect then ran away and hid from the responding officers who reported the wounded deputy. The suspect, who was later captured and subsequently admitted to shooting the deputy, said that he knew the deputy would arrest him, and he did not want to go to jail. He also indicated that he tried to shoot himself after the deputy had tased him, but then he shot the deputy and ran away.

Some will hurt and torture others for no other reason than to watch them suffer. Those are the purely evil ones. They care about no one but themselves and are just out to draw blood at the slightest provocation.

For example, on Monday, January 12, 1998, near the end of his shift, Deputy **Kyle Wayne Dinkheller** of the Laurens County Sheriff's Office (LCSO) in the state of Georgia encountered a speeding Toyota pickup truck near Dudley, Georgia, United States, which he clocked at around 98 miles per hour (158 km/h). The deputy pulled the truck over on Whipple Crossing Road, adjacent to Interstate 16. The traffic stop at first appeared to be routine, with both the deputy and Andrew Brannan exiting their vehicles and exchanging greetings. However, Brannan placed both hands into his pockets, at which point Dinkheller instructed him to remove his hands and keep them in plain view.

At this point, Brannan became belligerent and yelled at the deputy to shoot him. He then began to dance and wave his arms in the middle of the road. Dinkheller radioed the dispatcher for assistance and issued Brannan's commands to cease his behavior and approach the cruiser. When Brannan saw that Dinkheller was calling for other units, he aggressively ran toward the deputy. Dinkheller retreated while issuing commands and utilized his baton to keep Brannan at bay. On Dinkheller's dashcam video, Brannan shouted that he was a "Goddamned Vietnam combat veteran."

THE HARDEST LANGUAGE

Despite commands issued by Dinkheller, Brannan walked back to his pickup truck and drew an Iver Johnson M1 Carbine from underneath the driver's seat, taking cover near the driver's side door. Dinkheller positioned himself near his cruiser's passenger door, gave Brannan commands for approximately forty seconds before Brannan stepped away from his pickup truck, pointed his rifle at Dinkheller, and fired several shots. Dinkheller fired the first shot at Brannan but missed, leading some to speculate that it might have been a warning shot. Dinkheller did not strike the suspect initially and thus was forced to reload.

At this point, Brannan ran from his truck toward Dinkheller and began to fire again, hitting the deputy in exposed areas such as the arms and legs. Brannan then began to reload his weapon as the now-injured Dinkheller tried to position himself near his cruiser's driver side door and pleaded for his life. Brannan appeared to go back to his car to retreat before hearing another shot from Dinkheller. This enraged Brannan, who began advancing and firing at the deputy, hitting him numerous times. Before being disabled from gunfire, Dinkheller was able to inflict a gunshot wound to Brannan's stomach. Brannan shot Dinkheller nine times before he took careful aim, said, "Die fucker," and fired a final, fatal shot into Dinkheller's right eye. Brannan then retreated into his truck and fled the scene.

However, putting these extreme scenarios aside as well as others like it. Do you think it is possible to have a society where we, as officers of the law everywhere in the country, can use less force to discharge our duty every other day? Yes, it is very possible.

Carmelo Rodriguez

We can have a society where a simple everyday encounter between a law enforcement officer and a citizen does not have to degenerate into a confrontation like those, we see on tv and hear about in the news? We can have the number of officers and citizens' deaths through hostile confrontations reduced if we simply become more aware that force is only a last resort when dealing with people.

People are humans, and as humans, they have emotions triggered by our approach toward them. Suppose your first encounter with a citizen is to be hostile toward them; the likelihood of being hostile toward you increases. However, when in a non-life-threatening situation, and we approach the situation intelligently, we often get the cooperation of the people involved without the use of force.

Excessive force and police brutality don't just apply to cases of deadly force. Still, they can also find where injuries are relatively minor but resulted from unreasonable use of force. For example, there are situations where verbal statements like non-threatening requests or direct orders can quickly solve a problem instead of batons or chemical sprays.

The truth is, even recognizing that the right to make an arrest or investigatory stop carries with it the right to use some degree of physical coercion or threat by an officer, the degree of coercion or force used must be proportional to the threat and can only escalate in response to the threat.

For example, in an ideal situation, an officer should use the following graduated methods to diffuse a situation:

1. **Physical presence**: Using mere presence.

2. **Verbalization**: Using verbal statements, from non-threatening requests to direct orders.

3. **Empty-Hand Control**: Using physical bodily force through grabs, holds, tackles, etc.

4. **Less Lethal Methods**: Using weapons such as a baton, chemical sprays, Tasers, or police dogs.

5. **Lethal Force**: Using lethal weapons such as firearms.

To use force to be considered reasonable and compliant with the U.S. Constitution, the use of physical force must stop when the suspect is no longer poses a threat to life, body, or property; this also means that force becomes unnecessary with a successfully restrained suspect or the situation successfully de-escalated.

It is essential always to remember that the first approach to trying to resolve a situation is to use the de-escalation and communication skills taught earlier in this book. A little bit of force may be applied to enforce compliance if it is reasonable in the circumstance.

When considering the use of force in any situation, you must think of other alternative or available options before using the "last resort" if the situation does not change for the better. It is the last resort for a reason. This means that no officer is permitted to act forcefully toward a suspect when they pose no imminent danger to their lives.

In deciding whether the use of force will be appropriate in any situation, it is important to also consider the following before going ahead to act forcefully:

- The severity of the underlying crime or circumstances;
- Whether an immediate threat to your safety as an officer or others exists;
- If the suspect was actively resisting arrest or attempting to flee;
- If other alternatives were available; or
- If warnings have been provided.

This means that no officer is permitted to act forcefully toward a suspect until that officer thoroughly checks the above conditions.

Use of Force Justified.

Even though there is not a single, universally agreed-upon definition of the use of force, one that has been adopted and often used is that which was defined by the International Association of Chiefs of Police as the "amount of effort required by police to compel compliance by an unwilling subject."

This is to say that the use of force will be permitted and justifiable only:

- If it is reasonable in the circumstance;
- If it is necessary;
- If no more force used than necessary ; and
- If it is proportionate to the seriousness of the circumstances.

Reasonable in the circumstances: You may justify the use of force only if it is reasonable in the circumstance it is employed. The truth is circumstances may look alike, but they are seldom the same which means that officers must critically look at every circumstance on its merits before a judgment on the use of force is reached. Justification of force also means that one must consider the peculiarities of that particular circumstance before acting. You may need to consider the environment, whether it is crowded or secluded. You may also need to consider the suspect's age and sex, but most of all, you will need to consider if there is a weapon involved and, if yes, the type of weapon used.

Reasonably necessary: Another thing that justifies the use of force is if it is reasonably necessary for the situation. One must consider the type of harm they are trying to prevent before deciding if the use of force was justified or not.

These necessities may include situations where the suspect poses a:

- ➢ Threat to life
- ➢ Threat to limb/body
- ➢ Threat to property

For example, suppose a suspect is attempting to escape from an officer fighting with the suspect. In that case, it is reasonably necessary for the officer to use as much force as needed to constrain the suspect. However, the officer must endeavor not to use what would be considered deadly force such as a chokehold, strike to the head with a weapon, knee on the neck, as the situation may not require that.

No more force used than is necessary: As long as the force used in any circumstance is not in any way more than what is necessary, then consider it justifiable use of force. Using force greater than necessary is considered unlawful. For example, an officer using a lethal weapon like a gun on a suspect who has no weapon or poses no threat to life, limb, or property is using force more than is necessary and will be considered unlawful.

Proportionate in the circumstances: As long the action taken is proportionate to what an officer was trying to achieve. For example, it would not make any sense to shoot an unarmed citizen you already have pinned to the ground because you are trying to put them in cuffs. Even if the suspect is running away from an officer and has not posed an imminent threat to the officer or a citizen, then the suspect's shooting is not proportionate in the circumstances.

If there is a less forceful alternative to achieve a particular result, action taken may not be regarded as proportionate in the circumstances and will not be justified.

The police's authority to use force remains one of the most misunderstood powers granted to the government's representatives. Thus, we must apply every other less forceful strategy and alternatives in any situation that can be employed before things get escalated to the level where the use of force is our last resort.

Chapter 11

Community Policing

Evolution of Policing

To understand the origin of the perception people have about the police today, we'll need to go back in time to see what police officers' function was and how that has evolved since then. When we go back in time, we will discover that the police have always given off the vibe that portrays the "them versus us" mentality, especially within immigrant communities. Police were often projected as a tool used by the government to enforce oppressional laws in nature, especially to the minority communities of those days. The police's resentment began to build up in their heart even before they had any power to do anything about it.

For example, The Philadelphia police department is one of the oldest, if not the oldest police department in the nation today. It started as far back as the late 1700s. Then there were unpaid watchmen and constables walking up and down the street trying to keep the peace of the place, ensuring that doors are locked and living in a safe neighborhood as much as they should.

However, other police officers worked on plantations whose job was to track down slaves that had run away and have them brought back for punishment. Certainly, this deepened the fear people had for the police rather than the respect they should command.

People, especially those who lived in immigrant communities, never wanted anything to do with the police because of how they have positioned themselves and were perceived by them. Therefore, no matter the gravity of the crime committed and the information they have about the crime, they often will not call the police or volunteer information. Why? Because they have also been victims of police oppression themselves in one way or the other.

Now fast forward to the civil rights era; who was it that was enforcing the Jim Crow laws at the time? The Police. Who was it that the people encountered when they protested about any injustice done toward them? The police. The police sometimes used physical force to disperse the crowd of protesters and used sprays and other tools and tactics that may harm the protesters.

But should that have been police officers' response to protesters, especially within a society that touts itself as democratic? If you ask an average police officer today what their duty is in a democratic society like ours, you will most likely get the response that they are to enforce the law. While that may be true in some way, that is a very narrow view of our duty as police officers.

As officers of the law, everyone's constitutional rights are appropriately defended by our duty to go beyond enforcing the law to ensure that they are irrespective of race or creed. It goes beyond looking to drop crime rates in a community to ensure that the lives of those within that community, irrespective of whether accused of committing any crime or have genuinely committed a crime, is as protected as we do law-abiding citizens who are or may be the victims of the crime.

Think about it, if we as police officers believe and conduct ourselves in a manner consistent with the above, do you think we will be having the same problem we are having today or at least to the magnitude that it is occurring today? I do not think so.

Before now, I used to look at communities and wonder why there is a lot of mistrust, with people being afraid of the police. But, in retrospect, one can see that a lot of it has to do with police history in this country.

Police may have evolved since the Jim Crow and civil rights era; however, a lot is yet to change how citizens of this country perceive us. We still carry a lot of baggage from those eras into the present-day policing strategies. We use tactics and strategies that show us more as the law enforcers and not the defenders of everyone's constitutional rights.

Therefore, it becomes crucial that we begin to change that narrative through the instrumentality of strategies and tactics relevant to time, consciously deepening the people's involvement in policing and blurs the line between them versus us mentality, which is community policing.

Community Policing

Before we delve deeper into this topic, we must define community policing, giving us a clear understanding of what we are talking about in this chapter. Therefore, community policing, or community-oriented policing, is a policing strategy that focuses on building ties and working closely with community members to ensure lives and property are well preserved. It is a policing that sees the citizens' involvement as important and crucial to reducing crime and solving problems faced in that locality.

It can also be said to be a type of personalized policing where officers work in partnership with the citizens of a community to prevent, identify and solve crime-related issues that may be peculiar to that particular community. In other words, community policing is not just the regular or traditional policing where officers come and go or see themselves as different from the community. Still, this time is more involved in the happenings in that community. Here the police officers see themselves as a part of that community; thus, are genuinely committed and invested in seeing that the environment where they are called to serve is well protected and preserved.

In community policing, the same officer patrols and works in the same area permanently from a decentralized location to build relationships with the community through interactions with local agencies and its citizens to come up with strategies that will help reduce crime and disorder within that environment, which means that community policing is not reactive in its operation strategies but is predominantly proactive in that it seeks to prevent crimes even before they are hatched or executed.

This suggests that community policing is somewhat related to problem-oriented and intelligence-led policing, known to effectively reduce crime and raise the sense of security. It is also in contrast to the reactive policing strategy of the past.

With the advent of cars, telephones, and suburbanization in the early 20th century, the police force's modus operandi began to shift from what it used to be to what was more of a reactive stance toward combating crime. It was more focused on the fight against crime than it was on crime reduction, i.e., it was more reactive in its approach than it was proactive. For example, the focus was more on being efficient in responding to emergency calls as quickly as possible, relying on motor vehicle patrols to reducing crime and rotation of officers between different neighborhoods as a measure to prevent corruption.

This change in approach resulted in foot patrols being rare in some neighborhoods while also significantly altering the nature of police presence in some others, further widening the gap between officers of the law and their strategic interaction with the community they serve.

Carmelo Rodriguez

Community policing is an effective way to promote public safety and enhance citizens' quality of life in a community. It plays a vital role in the two defining policing elements, i.e., police-community relations and problem-solving.

When it comes to police-community relations, one key thing community policing does is that it fosters a deeper relationship between the police and the citizens by respectfully engaging and enlightening them about their roles in crime prevention, what to expect from the police, and what the police expects from them to serve them better.

Community policing puts a human face to policing against the "Non-human identity" of the entity police. For example, it is easier to say "f*** the police" when you have no human connections or relations with the officers involved than to say "f*** Deputy Rufus" when he has proven himself to be a valuable member of your community.

Community policing allows you to know more people in the community you serve, thereby fostering genuine relationships with them. Even better is if we live or stay around the community where we serve. After all, as a member of that community, you don't need to ask to know about the needs of the people living in that area because you experience what they experience firsthand.

In places where an officer's salary can permit, living in or around where you work also shows the people you police that you value them enough to live side by side with them. It shows them that you do not see them as different from you but as the same, which has a way to improve police-community relations.

In community policing, the community's average citizen's active involvement in ensuring that the policing of that area works, i.e., everyone, as long as you live or stay around that neighborhood, is responsible for safeguarding the welfare of that area. Meaning that policing goals in community policing are often expanded past the usual traditional policing goals so that the community's perception toward policing and police officers is positively affected.

When it comes to traditional policing, as we've often noticed, police officers are more or less tied to the dispatcher and rarely have time to get involved with the community because they are too busy responding to one call after another, thus making the police department look like an organization that separates itself from the city's infrastructure and city services.

However, when implementing community policing strategies in a place, police officers are not just tied to the dispatcher's voice but are positively involved in other community activities, thereby developing strong partnerships with the people of that place. Over time, this partnership can help the police find the underlying causes of crime within the neighborhood.

By getting the community involved in policing, the police have more resources available at their disposal to help them carry out their crime prevention function. Also, by acquainting themselves with the community members, officers are more likely to obtain valuable information about criminals and their activities. They are more likely to obtain a reliable evaluation of citizens' needs and their police expectations.

As has been stated before, community policing plays a significant part in police-community relations and problem-solving. The police must first form a great relationship with the neighborhood to collaborate with the community. The police must try to involve the neighborhood in its pursuit to control crime. Problem-solving identifies most community concerns and solutions. The objective is to lessen crime and disorder by diligently examining the attributes of concerns in communities and applying the most suitable problem-solving solutions.

COMMUNITY INVOLVEMENT

Community policing requires that the community be involved in the policing process of an area, which means that there can be no successful community policing without a community's active involvement. Therefore, here are a few ways a community can get involved in the community policing process.

As has been severally implied, community policing is only as good as the community's involvement in the process; this applies to community-based programs that are important in the service delivery in many communities.

In community policing, while officers deal with the criminal aspects of the process, some programs and projects must be carried out by the citizens of that community to help deter crime in their neighborhood, albeit with law enforcement officers' help.

Several programs can be implemented in partnership with the community when it comes to community policing. They include programs like "Neighborhood Watch, citizen police academies, citizen surveys, and the establishment of community policing units, etc. These programs must become a staple in many communities as long as the goal remains to steer crime away from residential areas. For example, programs like the National Night Out that symbolizes the unison in a neighborhood's drive to fight crime by leaving their outside lights on must become an essential part of community policing in different communities.

There are several other ways a citizen can get involved in community policing, one of which is, doing something as simple as making sure that an older man down the street makes it home safely from the grocery store to start their Neighborhood Watch program.

Neighborhood Watch teaches the residents of an area on how to detect suspicious activities and prevent crime from happening. Starting a Neighborhood Watch is very beneficial to the police and the community because the benefits of organizing and participating in a Neighborhood Watch program translate into a higher quality of life.

Another community-oriented program designed to make the youths feel good about the police hoping that they will later provide useful information about crime in their areas, is the D.A.R.E. Program. This particular program teaches young people and better equips them with the necessary skills needed to make well-informed choices and empower them to say no when tempted to use alcohol, tobacco, or drugs.

Another component of the D.A.R.E. program's design is to help students recognize the dangers of violence in their schools and community. You could say that the D.A.R.E. program "Humanizes" the police so that young people can begin to relate to officers as people and not some faceless entities. The D.A.R.E. program also allows students to see officers in a helping role and not just in an enforcement role and helps open up communication lines between law enforcement and youth officers who can serve as conduits to provide information beyond drug-related topics.

When critically looked at, one will realize that community policing not just a program but a philosophy. Suppose this philosophy of community policing is not understood correctly by those supposed to be involved. In that case, the community-oriented programs are bound to fail because the community-oriented programs are only a small part of making the community policing model work.

In the end, community policing will only work when the affected communities work together with the police and other governmental offices to ensure that it succeeds. The biggest obstacle that community policing and the community-based programs have to face is the idea of change, .i.e. officers have to change their mindset about policing, and citizens have to be willing to accept that change.

POLICE INVOLVEMENT

Since community policing focuses on a specific community's particular needs, there isn't any blanket schematic approach that works for all communities or neighborhoods. An approach that works in one jurisdiction may not be as effective in another due to the specific nature of the challenges they face in that community.

For example, using the same community policing approach for an area where gun violence seems to be the order of the day will seldom have any tangible impact in an area where drug use or prostitution is the bane of society.

Therefore, to adopt a community policing approach that works for the community it is called to serve, a police department must create its community policing style, reflecting the community's needs.

In their book, *"A vision of the future of policing in Canada,"* Normandeau & Leighton identified the following characteristics as essential for the success of any community policing effort:

- The mission of police officers as peace officers
- Community consultation
- A proactive approach to policing
- A problem-oriented strategy
- Crime prevention activities
- Interagency cooperation
- Interactive policing
- A reduction of the fear of victimization
- Development of police officers as generalists
- Decentralized police management

- Development of flatter organizational structures and accountability to the community

This invariably implies that adopting the philosophy of community policing by any police department involves a radical change in all organizational structure elements and processes.

Changing the Outlook

In addition to all said above, one of the radical changes that must occur for any community policing effort to be effective is the change in officers' outlook and mentality toward a community's citizens.

As police officers, we are primarily public servants before we are enforcers of the law; thus, we need to carry with us the mentality of service when dealing with people meaning that we need to move from carrying the warrior mentality as though we are at war with the citizens of a community to have the guardian mentality, one charged with the protection of those under his jurisdiction; this is very important because the way we see ourselves considerably drives how we behave toward others.

The police officers or their departments should not be seen as the thin blue line that separates good from evil—instead, seen as an essential thread woven throughout the communities we serve, helping to hold together the fabric of democracy.

Another essential thing we need to do as police officers are deal with the real issue of bias and encourage fair and impartial policing. In other words, we need to recognize that everyone has a bias of some kind, which could either be gender, racial, political affiliation, sexual orientation, etc. and that bias somewhat affects how we treat and respond to people.

Knowing that we all have them, it becomes important that we learn how to get them out of the way when dealing with community issues. We need to be sure we are not trying to superimpose our bias in the way we dispense justice in the communities where we serve. Nevertheless, the first key to dealing with it is recognizing that you have it and then consciously choose not to let it influence how you do your job.

As police officers, we need to start showing more respect for the communities we serve irrespective of their bias dictates. We need to understand the culture of the place because it is everything and then learn how to work around it. One other thing that we need to do is to learn the lingo of the place or the unofficial language in the streets of the community where we serve because it makes it easy for us to communicate and perhaps relate more and understand what people around that area are feeling or are trying to say to us.

For example, being a Latino raised in a large city and in the ghetto, I can easily understand the lingos or the language of the streets within the Latino community; hence, I'm able to relate better with them because not only do I understand their speech but I also understand the non-verbal cultural cues within the area.

We also need to realize that we all "bleed red blood" and that we are first humans before we had on that uniform as police officers. Therefore, we must do everything to ensure we treat people with dignity and respect because after all is said and done, their honor is all that they have left, and will be willing to fight you to the death to preserve it.

Chapter 12

Emotional Intelligence

What is Emotional Intelligence?

Emotional Intelligence is the quality that enables us to confront with patience, insight, and imagination the many problems that we face in our significant relationship with ourselves and with other people. It can also be said to be the ability to understand, use, and manage your own emotions in positive ways to relieve stress, communicate effectively, empathize with others, overcome challenges, and defuse conflict.

Defined in some quarters as the capability of individuals to recognize their own emotions and those of others, discern between different feelings and label them appropriately, use emotional information to guide thinking and behavior, and manage and adjust emotions to adapt to environments or achieve one's goal(s)

Emotional intelligence may sound strange to some people because we see intelligence as a general quality of either being book smart or streetwise. We often don't know or consider the other variation of intelligence, which has to do with understanding and perceiving, and dealing with emotions and emotional situations with grace.

In fact, in many settings, today, including work, academic, or business setting, a high IQ is considered as one of the most desirable personality qualities. People employ I.Q. Tests for many purposes such as selection, diagnosis, and evaluation in many parts of society today because of the claims that it is the single most accurate predictor of individual performance at school and on the job, but is it?

At different points in our lives, I'm sure we have seen people who have high IQ scores and are presumed to be intelligent do things that often leave us asking if they were brilliant when it comes to human relations or interaction. When someone is said to be ingenious but seems to make a mess of their personal lives or have through their groundbreaking ideas acquired a fortune but are restless and sad or are powerful, and at the helm of affairs at a corporation but intolerant or bland, that is a pointer to the fact that they lack in the form of intelligence that their IQ level cannot measure, emotional intelligence.

While every other sort of intelligence indicates the ability to navigate well a particular set of challenges, be it mathematical, linguistics, technical, commercial, etc., emotional intelligence helps us navigate our emotions effectively, being able to label and manage them correctly, rather than being managed by them. Emotional intelligence helps us in manage our response in our day to day dealing with other people, ensuring that we do not blow over the top no matter the situation.

Emotional intelligence also helps us interpret others' emotional responses or actions toward us correctly without being as judgmental as we would have been if we were emotionally unintelligent. For example, emotional intelligence helps us recognize that the explosive outburst of a customer in a queue might be a disguised plea for help or her uneasiness provokes a pregnant woman's angry complaint.

Emotional intelligence helps us as cops look beyond the surface of a person's response to the emotional undertone behind it. i.e., emotional intelligence helps us become sensitive to others' moods and emotions to understand what may be going on with that person beyond the surface.

Humans are naturally emotional beings because of the way our brains are wired. Thus, we are more likely to react first to an event in an emotional way than we are prone to respond logically. We do not have control over this process; however, we control the thoughts that follow after those emotions, leading to actions if we are emotionally intelligent.

For example, as officers of the law, we are sometimes faced with the task of taking into custody someone who is refusing arrest. In an attempt to enforce that arrest, they unintentionally hit us in the face with their fist. This can sometimes lead to a feeling of anger within us to which our natural emotional reaction may be to hit them back immediately. However, when we're emotionally intelligent, we will most likely look past the attack to our face and not retaliate with blows to their head or body and then use whatever intelligent strategy at our disposal to ensure they get taken into custody.

Due to the natural biases we have as humans, some situations tend to tick us off and react in certain ways. These situations are called trigger events. A trigger event can be a situation that elicits a particular type of emotional response from us and is shaped by our personal history or experiences with similar situations. For example, seeing someone beat a traffic stop sign can be a trigger event for you, and it causes us to react angrily at the driver of the car because you have had an experience in your life where you lost someone dear to you because of a drunk driver who beat the stop sign. However, as your emotional intelligence skills grow, you'll learn to identify your triggers and practice productive ways of responding that will eventually become your new normal.

When it comes to his feelings or emotions, an emotionally intelligent person is the number one skeptic of their emotions, i.e., they intentionally refuse to trust the first impulse their emotions generate or their feelings' inherent wisdom because they know that what they are feeling could be a mask for another underlying issue with which they may need to deal. They know that hatred may mask itself as love, and anger may be a cover for sadness.

THE HARDEST LANGUAGE

Studies have shown that people with high emotional intelligence have greater mental health, job performance, and leadership skills. Before this was established as a fact via research and scientific study, those qualities were, in the past, attributed to people who are perceived to have general intelligence and specific personality traits rather than emotional intelligence.

In their book Emotional Intelligence 2.0, the authors Travis Bradberry and Jean Greaves alluded to the fact that *"When emotional intelligence was first discovered, it served as the missing link in a peculiar finding: people with the highest levels of intelligence (IQ) outperform those with average IQs just 20 percent of the time, while people with average IQs outperform those with high IQs 70 percent of the time. This anomaly threw a massive wrench into what many people had always assumed was the source of success—IQ. Scientists realized there must be another variable that explained success above and beyond one's IQ, and years of research and countless studies pointed to emotional intelligence (EQ) as the critical factor."*

Emotional intelligence distinguishes those who get easily crushed with failure from those who know how to take their failure as an opportunity to learn a new approach and start again. Imagine the emotional strength it would have required for someone to fail 99 times and keep going. The emotionally intelligent appreciate the role of well-handled pessimism within the overall economy of a good life.

Emotional Intelligence is not an inborn talent. It's merely a result of education, i.e., education on how to interpret our emotions, where they arise from, how our childhood or past experiences influence us and how we might best navigate our fears and wishes. Emotional intelligence is a learnable skill.

In a 21st century policing system, emotional intelligence training should be routinely taught to officers from time to time and not relegated to what we can only teach young officers coming out from police academies. Every officer ought to learn and master emotional intelligence even before we had the opportunity to make too many mistakes.

Permit to say here that we have not taken emotional intelligence training seriously enough that there seems to be an increasing number of police clashes reported in the media. Emotional intelligence training is more than something that should occur in police classrooms at the hands of teachers and come to an end once we leave those training ground. It should be continuous, and one central vehicle for the transfer of emotional intelligence is culture.

When we respond to emotional situations intelligently, a culture in every police department in the nation gradually becomes the new norm against the way some officers tend to react to emotionally charged situations. The truth is, we will rarely progress as a people and in our relations to the citizens of our country until we have accepted the challenges and opportunity of properly educating ourselves on emotional intelligence.

Why Emotional Intelligence is Essential for the Police

As officers of the law, we often endure a great deal of stress due to facing critical, often life-threatening situations regularly. When not correctly dealt with, this stress can become chronic, leading us to experience a total burn out, emotional exhaustion, a decline in personal accomplishment, or even depersonalization of ourselves from our job. It may sometimes make us more fearful, aggressive, and even anxious about our day-to-day activities than it ought to; this invariably affects how they relate and interact with members of a community where they serve.

Today, more than ever, the clashes between law enforcement officers and the general public seem to be on the increase because of the media attention such issues are enjoying and the emotional outburst such incidents whip up. Hardly will you turn on the news without hearing of a case of racial profiling, excessive use of force, discourtesy, lack of empathy, etc. involving the police. And when properly analyzed, most of these cases can be traced back to the officer's inability to control their emotions or their lack of emotional intelligence.

Think about this; police departments are laden with responding to calls for service and investigating crimes after they have been committed. However, that department could have trained more of its officers to handle their emotions skillfully or become better, emotionally intelligent officers?

Some officers are assigned to field operations within a police department, so they respond to calls for service. In contrast, some others are assigned to investigative services, that is, to investigate crimes after they have been committed. Field operations officers become responsible for the initial response to calls such as domestic violence, sexual assaults, and violent crimes such as aggravated assaults and homicide. In contrast, the Investigators become responsible for the investigation's long-term outcome, such as conducting lengthy interviews and identifying suspects, exposing both groups of people to these emotionally charged situations.

All these can be emotionally traumatizing for the law enforcement officers not trained in emotional intelligence. In most cases, they are expected to endure the process and repress whatever emotions they feel or leave it unacknowledged. However, studies have shown that this is a very wrong way of dealing with emotions because it will eventually "Leak out" in the long run and affect how an officer relates and interacts with his environment.

Some officers become "Cold hearted" while others try to suppress the emotions experience an outburst even in situations that do not require such a response. For example, officer Mike is coming from a scene where an armed robber has just shot a shop owner, then called to another scene where a college student was caught shoplifting some items from a mobile phone store.

The officer, with his emotions still flying high from the previous scene, gets to the store. Without such interactions, he tries to arrest the college student who initially tried to resist until the officer brought out his gun, pointing right to his head and threatening to shoot him.

To the people watching from a distance, officer Mike has responded in a way that did not commiserate with the offense committed. However, no one knows that officer Mike has just witnessed a traumatizing situation where he watched a father shot in the chest because of the little change he had in his drawer. His emotions are still out of control before arriving at the scene.

In the example above, if officer Mike had been trained in the skill of emotional intelligence or were at least emotionally intelligent, he would have been able to isolate the two events and process his emotions carefully and correctly even before arriving at the scene of the shoplifting incident.

Component of Emotional Intelligence

Daniel Goleman, a science journalist, and psychologist of international repute, carried out extensive research on Emotional Intelligence and discovered that there are five main components to Emotional Intelligence, and he described them as follows:

Self-awareness

Self-awareness refers to a person's ability to recognize and understand their own moods, emotions, drives, and how they affect them and their performance. Knowing what you are feeling, why you are feeling that way, and how it helps or hurts what you are trying to do or achieve. For example, in our previous example, if Officer Mike were self-aware, he would have recognized that he was still feeling angry coming from the previous crime scene and thus should self-regulate before getting to the phone store.

Self-awareness helps you see yourself exactly how others see you, so you do not have an exaggerated view of yourself, thereby aligning your self-image with a larger reality. When you are self-aware, you have a clear sense of your strengths and weaknesses and can work in line with them.

In other words, self-awareness helps you build a realistic self-confidence in yourself so that when you speak about your visions or goals, you speak candidly and authentically.

Self-regulation

Self-regulation refers to a person's ability to control or redirect disruptive emotional impulses and moods. Self-regulation is the ability to allow yourself time to think through a situation before responding to it rather than just acting on your emotional impulses. From a neuroscientific perspective, you can frequently observe this skill or lack it by watching people's response time to action.

For example, if an officer is in rapid-fire mode responding to what you say in less than or in about half a second, it is very likely that they do not give conscious thought to what is said to them.

A person who knows how to self-regulate possess

- An inclination toward reflection and thoughtfulness
- Acceptance of uncertainties and change
- Integrity –specifically, the ability to say no to impulsive urges

People with this self-regulation ability will frequently demonstrate trustworthiness, integrity, comfort, and openness to change.

THE HARDEST LANGUAGE

Internal motivation

Internal motivation deals with a person's ability to continue to work because of an inner vision of what is important, curiosity and desire for learning and development, or a drive beyond external rewards such as money or status. It has the strength to keep going even when there are several obstacles on the way.

Internal motivation often shows up in a person as a strong desire to achieve set goals, a drive to take initiatives, and commit to complete a task irrespective of how difficult it may seem. Internally motivated people are not there for the money – even though appreciated – but are there for the general good it will bring.

For example, an internally motivated teacher or police officer may not care about the money or a promotion – even though this will be highly appreciated – but will continue to show up ready and motivated to work each day.

Empathy

Empathy refers to our ability to understand other people's emotions and reactions. Achieving empathy is only possible when we are self-aware because we must understand ourselves first before we can understand another.

Empathy deals with our capacity to understand others' emotional makeup, i.e., it deals with our capacity to perceive others' moods and emotions, becoming genuinely interested in what they are going through and understanding their perspective on the situation.

Empathy focuses on our ability to treat others according to their emotional reactions and includes building and maintaining relationships with those we come into contact with daily.

Social skills

True emotional understanding involves more than just being self-aware and showing empathy to others to be able to put this information to work in your day-to-day dealings with people. Therefore, social skills refer to our ability to manage relationships, build networks, pick up on jokes and sarcasm, find common ground, and build rapport with the people around us.

This skill is vital when trying to initiate change, persuade a person or people to action, and work effectively within a team or with a partner, which means that social skills are a very important skill to have when it comes to community policing. With it, the police can build a beneficial relationship and connection with the community where they serve.

Importance of Emotional Intelligence for an officer

Emotional intelligence is an essential skill that every law enforcement officer must have because it, among other things:

- Promote work-life balance.
- Improves officer's empathy for others.
- Promotes better stress management.
- Prevents Burnout amongst police officers.

Promotes Work-Life Balance

Emotional intelligence helps police officers deal effectively with the emotional demands of the day-to-day stress they face in their field of work. It also helps them maintain a balance between their professional lives and their personal lives, so there is no spillover of a work-related issue to the home and home-related issue to work. In other words, it means that it helps them effectively separate the two while also maintaining a balance between them.

Improves Officer's Empathy for Other

Due to the number of people and issues police officers get to encounter every day or every week, they may sometimes forget that they are different humans with different real issues, thereby treating them as just a number in the statistics or as just one in the number of similar cases.

However, with emotional intelligence, police officers can treat everyone they encounter with respect and empathy; showing them kindness and understanding for their situation thus making them feel safe and increasing their confidence in the law enforcement officers in their neighborhood.

Emotional intelligence also helps officers act rationally so they don't blow situations that can have devastating consequences out of proportion by their emotional outbursts.

Promotes Better Stress Management

Emotionally intelligent police officers can adequately manage stress and withstand adverse situations like being shot at or losing a partner without falling apart or caving in under the weight of such loss.

Officers with high levels of emotional intelligence can self-regulate and deal with stressful situations without losing an ounce of optimism or positivity, even in the face of a challenge. They are the type of officers who are just recovering from adversity and are eager to get back in the field of play.

An emotionally intelligent officer understands that certain things are beyond their control, making it easy for them to practice, thereby refraining from impulsive and explosive behavior.

Prevents Burnout Among Police Officers

One of the long-term effects of stress amongst police officers is that it leads to burnout, which causes many to commit suicide or develop PTSD. However, research has shown that law enforcement officers' burnout rate will lower if they can become emotionally intelligent. Officers with higher levels of emotional intelligence have developed the added ability to understand, perceive, and manage emotions, making them less likely to experience burn out.

Therefore, officers of the law must go through emotional intelligence training from time to time. This training helps improve the way they relate with the citizens and helps preserve their own lives.

Conclusion

In conclusion, law enforcement's emotional intelligence is not an abstract concept of trying to downplay our authorities like law enforcement officers. Instead, it is the demonstration of competencies that constitute self-awareness, self-regulation, internal motivation, Empathy, and social skills at appropriate times and in ways that is sufficient to be useful in any given situation.

Therefore, the key to making a tangible change to law enforcement's current state as it relates to police officers interfacing effectively with the citizens is to operationalize emotional intelligence and teach it to all officers irrespective of their number of years of service.

ABOUT THE AUTHOR

Carmelo Rodriguez is a certified life coach and motivational speaker with a background in law enforcement and crisis intervention. Carmelo has helped numerous individuals from all backgrounds. He talks of life transitions from low motivation, unfulfilled potential, and chronic self-doubt to achieving their vision and reaching their utmost success both personally and professionally. He applies a *strengths-based approach* to build upon client attributes rather than the traditional method of an excess focus on "fixing" personal flaws.

Carmelo's philosophy is that people achieve recovery and progress in their self-development by gaining awareness of their self-destructive patterns and perceived barriers that have prevented them from pursuing their goals and actualizing their best 'self.' However, the real work lies in the process of learning to see your positive traits and apply these unique abilities in your daily life. Discussions with Carmelo will help you learn to be no longer discouraged or debilitated by past failures and, instead, conceptualize your life experiences as integral parts of your growth and progress. Many of us have been taught that failure is to be avoided at all costs; Carmelo will show you how *failure is simply a threshold*—beyond it lies the greatest experiences and opportunities of your life. His intrinsic passion for life coaching is evidenced in his energy toward his work and his utmost commitment to the development of each client he serves.

Carmelo works alongside his clients to develop an individually tailored action plan and specific strategies to initiate and maintain change. He believes that successful attainment requires clear focus, burning motivation, and diligence toward the required practical action steps. Carmelo can reach life coaching clients and military personnel anywhere through his virtual online speeches and one-to-one classes. He offers crisis intervention services with his keen sense of various de-escalating conflict sources, from suicide risks to domestic violence or substance abuse.

Carmelo is a four-time author and will be appearing on the upcoming reality show *Behind the Badge*. He holds a B.A. in Criminal Justice, as well as an MBA. He has completed dozens of post-graduate certifications in crisis intervention, conflict management, and corporate crisis management. He is a Certified Life Coach and Confidence Coach, and he is currently a student at Harvard Business School, where he is completing coursework in Executive Negotiations. He is a United States Army combat veteran, and he is presently designing a self-development program for military service members transitioning to civilian life. Despite Carmelo's extensive academic and professional background, he considers himself a continuous learner. He believes that his journey as a coach and public speaker has brought immense meaning and satisfaction to his life.

OTHER BOOKS BY CARMELO RODRIGUEZ

Dead Soldier: A Story of the Living

We Are Human Too: Thin Blueline Stories from DC

Race Against Your Alarm Clock

THE HARDEST LANGUAGE

Carmelo Rodriguez

www.ingramcontent.com/pod-product-compliance
Lightning Source LLC
Chambersburg PA
CBHW071502040426
42444CB00008B/1460